What My Dog Taught Me About God

*Reconnecting With God's Love
and Emerging from a Spiritual Wilderness*

by
Fran A.Wood

Lemon Tree Publishing
Bradenton, Florida
www.booksbylemontree.com

Library of Congress Control Number 2007906157

ISBN 978-0-9797591-0-9

Printed in the United States of America

MEMORIAL

In memory of:

My "Daddy"
Robert Charles Arnold
10/03/1912 - 01/01/1984

My "Mama"
Mary Ovella Grace Arnold Borleis
06/02/1919 - 11/15/2001

My "Dad" (stepfather)
Herbert Henry Borleis
10/26/1906 - 08/26/2001

In the final analysis, what counts most in a life is not the dates that appear on one's gravestone but the dash between the dates. Thank you Daddy and Mama and Dad for making your "dash" count in my life.

He is your friend, your partner,
your defender, your dog.
You are his life, his love, his leader.

He will be yours, faithful and true,
to the last beat of his heart.

You owe it to him to be worthy of such devotion.
Anonymous

Acknowledgments

This book would not have been possible without the consistent support and the wise counsel of my husband Jim. Thank you, Honey, for your research, your tireless assistance and proofreading, your patience, your encouragement and most of all for your constant love.

Thanks also to my sons, Carl Harbuck, Alan Harbuck and Jeffrey Wood for their love, support and advice.

What is life without good friends who come alongside in times of need? I especially want to thank my friend Robert K. Goddard, author of *Upper House Conspiracy,* for his expert advice and counsel.

Other friends helped with support and encouragement, with theological insights, with proofreading and with suggestions. I am especially grateful to my pastor John Nolte and his wife Gaydean for their encouragement and insights and to my dear friends Bobbie Belcher, Sharon Dingeldein, Jan Bocchino, Mimi Ragsdale and Brenda Yanofsky for proofreading and recommendations.

I fear that I may have failed to mention someone. If so, please know that it was inadvertent and the fault of my aging memory. To all of you dear ones who helped please accept my heartfelt gratitude.

Contents

———

INTRODUCTION

I had reached a terrible place in my spiritual walk. I was wandering in the wilderness—again. I was well acquainted with the wilderness, having been there often, usually as the result of some life-altering event. One such time followed the death of my father in 1984, after an extended illness. I was profoundly impacted by his suffering, and as a "daddy's girl," I felt the loss deeply when he went home to the Lord. But, rather than reaching out to the God of all comfort, I turned my face to the wall and then wandered off into the wilderness. It took me a long time to return.

Throughout life I have found that I follow an all-too-familiar pattern in dealing with trials. I go into the wilderness and hang out alone and depressed, refusing comfort—from God, from family, from friends, from anyone or anything whatsoever. I suspect that I began this pattern when I was only about eighteen months old. I don't remember the particular incident that follows here, but my daddy remembered it well and told it to me often. He would smile as he recounted the story, but the smile couldn't mask the painful nostalgia in his tone and the slight mist in his eyes.

The year was 1945, and Daddy was home on leave from

the Navy. Being too young to remember ever having seen him before, I wanted nothing to do with him. Daddy always had a soft spot for children, so it especially grieved him to be shunned by his own infant daughter. He plied me with candy, cookies, and a toy or two, and eventually won me over. Soon we were inseparable, and he became my hero. As his constant companion, I clung to him everywhere he went—just Daddy and me. I'm sure my sister, Sylvia, also came along with us, but with my arms locked around his neck, my eyes were only on Daddy.

Alas, the day came when he had to return to duty, and I didn't understand why I had to let him go. My infantile mind couldn't comprehend war and service to country. I was inconsolable. Daddy wanted to give me a parting embrace, but I stood stiffly in the corner, face to the wall, sobbing, and vehemently waving off anyone's attempt to comfort me. Daddy left with a lump in his throat and tears in his eyes.

Apparently, that incident started a pattern that has continued throughout my life. I call it my "wilderness journey." Whenever something goes terribly wrong, I don't run to my Father God for comfort. Instead, I go off into an emotional wasteland where I try desperately not to feel the pain.

The wilderness journey which forms the backdrop of this book was brought about by the deaths of both my mother and my stepfather, within a few weeks' time in 2001—the 9/11 terrorist attack occurring in the middle of that time. I was left feeling confused, lost and abandoned. Intellectually, I knew that God had not forsaken me, and I longed to reconnect emotionally, yet the wilderness engulfed my soul, and I felt powerless in its hold.

It was during this spiritual badlands interval that God gave me a very special gift in the person of a tiny puppy whom I call "Bandit." As I began caring for Bandit and his needs, God began to reveal His special care and love for me in ways that I had never understood before. As remarkable as it may seem, God started teaching me through a puppy.

Bandit is now four years old, and I continue to learn from him daily as my heart swells with ever increasing love for him—not because of anything he does, but just because he *IS*. He doesn't have to earn my love. I love him because he is. That's all. He doesn't need to *DO* anything. He just needs to *BE*. I am reminded that God created us as human BEings, *not* as human DOings. He loves us just because we *ARE*.

I love Bandit simply because of the fellowship I enjoy with him. And I love him because he seems to love me. He seems to love being in my presence just sitting and "communing" with me—in whatever ways a dog can commune with a human. I fancy that my relationship with God is in some ways analogous. He is high above me, and His language and wisdom greatly surpass mine, yet we have a line of communication that transcends our differences and celebrates our sameness.

Having lived through a childhood fraught with the need to be accepted and just to be loved, I have come to the marvelous realization that God loves me regardless. I am His and He is mine and His banner over me is love. (Song of Solomon 6:3 and 2:4.)

As you read through this book, I pray that you will come to see the Father's great love for you in a new and fresh way that ministers to your heart and spirit right where you are in your own spiritual journey.

Chapter One
Bandit Comes Into My Life

Deliver me from the sword,
My precious life from the *power of the dog.*
Psalm 22:20 [Emphasis mine.]

If you are not *planning* to get a dog, do not under any circumstances, go *looking* at puppies! There. You have been warned.

One day on an outing with my husband, I ventured into a music store, and the owner happened to have his little dog there that day—a honey-colored, bouncy little fluff ball named Otis. Otis greeted me standing on his hind legs holding his paws up. Still standing erect, he danced around gleefully as he excitedly worked his paws up and down inviting me to play. This was my introduction to the sweet, unpredictable, loving, playful, joyful, incredible breed called Shih Tzu. (Unfortunate nomenclature, which must be pronounced carefully! It's "*sheets*-zu, Not . . . well, not what you might have been

1

thinking.) Captivated by this little Shih Tzu, I often thought and talked of him for weeks afterwards.

Still infatuated with Otis, I happened to look in the classifieds one day and saw an ad for Shih Tzu puppies. (First mistake!) Why I was looking in the "pets" section of the classifieds is fodder for further psychological analysis. I wasn't looking for a dog. . . I didn't want a dog. . . yet, the paper was open to "pets". . . and I didn't look through the "cats" section. I went straight to "dogs"!

The ad gave a phone number to call in order to see the puppies. "What harm can it do to look?" I thought. Otis, a full-grown Shih Tzu, had been adorable. Just imagine how sweet a Shih Tzu puppy must be! Intending only to look at the puppies, I dialed the number and feigned interest in purchasing one.

I also had an ulterior motive. At the time, my husband Jim and I were marketing a wonderful stress alleviating formula which had been found to be particularly helpful to both humans and animals in competitions such as athletic events, talent shows or (you got it) pet shows! My plan was to look at the puppies and talk to the breeder about our product for herself and her dogs. Thus, I could see some cute puppies and make a business call at the same time.

I drove past the house but didn't stop. I felt like a criminal—deceiving this unsuspecting woman about my real motives. So I passed on by the house, having made up my mind not to stop just as it came into view. But she was out in the front yard with the puppies—and they were darling! I turned around, went back and stopped. (Second mistake!)

The puppies were delightful. They bounded around the yard hardly any taller than the grass they were in. I spotted a particularly charming one. He was brown and white, with an enchanting little face, and soft, soulful eyes. I picked him up. (Third mistake!) He nestled his little face against my neck and he sighed—a deep, longing puppy sigh. I was hooked!

I called my husband—who (wisely) had not been in favor of my going on this venture.

"I think I have to get this puppy," I said, the little creature still nestled against my neck. Jim's response was less than enthusiastic.

"You know how much trouble he would be and how frequently we travel," he pointed out with typical male pragmatism.

"I know, but he's just so *sweet.* I don't think I can leave him here," I lamented.

"Well, it's up to you," he said in a resigned tone that conveyed, "I know you want to do this. So I might as well go along with you." I was somewhat surprised that Jim gave in so readily. We had both been resolute about "no pets" ever since our previous dog, Charlie, had died several years earlier. Perhaps Jim relented in light of my fragile emotional state during the past year following the deaths of both my mother and stepfather. Maybe he thought that a new puppy would help fill the hole in my aching heart.

Since the puppy was too young to leave his mother, I put a deposit on him and left. I had to wait two agonizing weeks before I could go back and get him. I say "agonizing" because I had noticed that the woman's toddler son was not particularly gentle with the puppies, and I imagined my little guy suffering at the hands of this child for the entire two weeks. Plus, she kept the puppies in a cage in the garage, and I felt sorry for them in such a "cruel" environment. Please realize that this was a private breeder and the pups' confines in her home were leagues ahead of a "puppy mill." These dogs were actually in a palace by comparison, but still I fretted over my little fellow.

At last, the day came when I could pick him up. He was dirty and smelled of urine and feces from being caged with his siblings. Nevertheless, because he was frightened, I held him close on the ride home, ignoring the stench. I continued to hold him close even though his fright caused him to wet himself—and me! My introduction to "unconditional love" for this tiny beast. As soon as we arrived home, the first order of the day was to change my wet clothes and give him a bath!

Looking back on that moment, I can see that from the beginning my relationship with this little creature has, in some small ways, mirrored my Heavenly Father's care of me. I chose the puppy, I brought him unto myself—even though he reeked—and then I cleaned him up. He was dirty and smelly, and I washed him clean. My Heavenly Father chose me out of the cage of sin that enslaved me, and I came to Him all dirty from sin and with the odors and cares of this world all over me. He gently took me, held me close—in spite of the stench—and then carefully washed me clean.

Obviously, not everything about having a dog is analogous to how God the Father relates to His children, but in raising my dog, I have come to recognize many similarities that have helped me see more clearly just how unconditional the Father's love is. And, just as I had bought Bandit, He bought me at a price—the life of His only Son.

As I have endeavored to raise this little guy—whom we call "Bandit"—I have continued to see some comparisons between my unconditional love for him and the Father's unlimited, unwavering love for me. Bandit, as it turns out, is definitely *not* an "Otis." Bandit is a very "alpha" male with a mind and strong will of his own—which he demonstrated from the get-go—when, the fourth night he spent with us, he bit me on the face! Suffice it to say that Bandit has been a challenge and a joy all at the same time.

Now, more than four years from the day I first fell in love with him, he sits at my feet as I write this. He has just gotten up from his night's rest and wandered into my office and is waiting for his breakfast. He looks at me from time to time with expectant eyes reminding me that he hasn't been fed yet today. Still, he has no doubt that I will soon feed him. He is not concerned at all about receiving his "daily bread" from this person who loves him—flaws and all.

Chapter Two

The Spiritual Vacuum
and How I Got There

Turn [me] back to You, O Lord,
and [I] will be restored;
Renew [my] days as of old.
Lamentations 5:21

From the day Bandit came into my life, he unwittingly began teaching me about God and about His abundant and unconditional love for me. I had been in a spiritual vacuum ever since my mother and my stepfather had both passed away (within eleven weeks of each other) the previous year. They had both started a decline that became quite noticeable in the latter part of the year 2000. I first noticed my mother's physical weakness when we picked her and Dad up for lunch one day and I observed that she had trouble getting up into our van. At eighty-one, my mother was as nimble as a squirrel. She always sprang right up into our van. This day, however, I saw that she struggled to get up onto the seat, having to get on her knees in the floor first. Alarmed, I asked her about it, and she brushed it off. "My legs have been feeling a little weak," she explained, and she dismissed it as something to be expected at her age. I wasn't convinced. It seemed to have come on quite suddenly.

My stepfather had been declining mentally for the previous two years. At ninety-four, he was quite a bit older than my mother. His memory had become so poor that he would often ask the same question over and over again—not remembering that he had just asked and received an answer. Mother's physical weakness was disturbing. It most assuredly meant that they would not be able to continue to live alone in their own home.

A year or so prior, I had considered the possibility of moving them closer to me so that I could keep a better eye on them. They lived about an hour's drive away. Our family was not in agreement on such a move, however, so I resigned myself to the fact that other arrangements were going to have to be made at some point. Although our family disagreed on how best to help our parents, there was one thing on which we were in complete accord. We wanted Mother and Dad to be safe and at least content—if outright happiness were, in fact, too lofty a goal at this point in their lives. I lived in constant anxiety knowing that inevitable change was coming.

There came a defining moment when Mother called me

in a panic.

"There's a man on the bathroom floor, and I can't get him up!" she exclaimed.

Shocked, I asked, "Who is it?"

"I can't remember his name," she cried.

It suddenly occurred to me that she was talking about her husband of—at that time—about thirteen years. "Why can't she remember his name?" I thought in alarm.

I asked if Dad could speak, and Mother assured me that he could, that he seemed all right except that he couldn't get himself up off the floor, and she was unable to lift him.

Because Dad had fallen a few times before, I knew that a call to 911 would land him in the hospital. There, disoriented and frightened, he would have to be restrained, *i.e.,* tied in bed. He would be there for days until medical staff finally decided that he could return home. (My interpretation: The number of days Medicare would cover were exhausted.)

I couldn't bear to see that happen to him again. So I told Mother to put a blanket around him, get him a pillow and keep him comfortable. And we sped to Port Charlotte.

We arrived to find Dad comfortable on the bathroom floor and fretting that he couldn't get up. We helped him up, and he was fine. But Mother was another story. She looked as though she had been in an automobile accident. Her arms were awfully bruised, as was her face, and she had a black eye.

Reading this, you probably immediately jumped to the conclusion that Dad had hit her. He hadn't. And he was such a sweet, gentle, man that it didn't even occur to us to wonder. It turned out that she had fallen over a stationary exercise bicycle in their bathroom. To my knowledge, they hadn't used the exercycle in years, but they never bothered to get rid of it. As Mother had struggled trying to pull Dad to his feet, she had lost her grip and fallen into the bike, and it had done a number on her arms and face.

We assumed that the shock of her collision with the exercycle had caused her to momentarily forget Dad's name. Regardless, it was disconcerting. As her health—both mental and physical—continued to deteriorate rapidly, I often thought back to that day and wondered why we had not taken Mother to the emergency room. At the time, though, she seemed fine, just bruised.

Looking back, I realize that the events of that day were the turning point marking the commencement of the last chapter of my mother and stepfather's lives. It was definitely the beginning of our search for a safe environment for them.

There was a lot of distressing family friction before our parents were eventually settled (or so we thought) into a very nice, beautiful assisted living facility (ALF) which had recently been built about two miles from their home in Port Charlotte, Florida. It was a lovely place which looked like a manor home with a huge front porch full of rocking chairs. I would often arrive to find Mother and Dad rocking on the front porch enjoying the warm Florida sun. The dining room was elegant and served excellent, tasty food. My parents seemed to be acclimating and were starting to make friends with some of the other residents.

It quickly became obvious, however, that something was drastically wrong with Mother when she continued to rapidly lose strength and mobility. It turned out that she had a subdural hematoma. Perhaps it had happened the day she fell into the exercise bike or perhaps she had sustained it in one of her many other falls. We had learned later that she had been having something similar to transient ischemic attacks (which cause momentary loss of consciousness), and had fallen several times. Surgery for the subdural hematoma failed, and merely initiated an even more rapid decline.

Within two months of Mother and Dad having moved into that lovely facility, it became necessary to move them into a nursing home—a not-so-lovely facility, but one that was very clean and offered excellent care. I could write a book on choosing a nursing home. Suffice it to say that one of the most important considerations is the patient/staff ratio. This partic-ular home had a really good (four to one) ratio—and it was affordable. And they agreed to keep Mother and Dad in the same room so that they didn't have to be separated. Many homes would have separated them and put Dad into an Alzheimer's unit. The area they were in had both regular and Alzheimer's patients and was secure (locked with ample overseeing staff), so Dad didn't have to go to a separate section.

I have emblazoned on my mind the day Jim and I had to go to the ALF, load my parents into a handicap transport van, and take them to the nursing home located in Bradenton, Florida—about an hour's drive from Port Charlotte, but, thankfully, only about five miles from my home. They said tearful goodbyes to staff members and to the few friends they had been able to make during their short stay. It was a pitiful scene, and I struggled for composure but managed to hold back my own tears as we left.

I rode in the back of the van with Mother and Dad. Jim followed in our car. I sat by my mother's wheelchair and held her as she sobbed softly. Dad wondered aloud why Mother was crying. His mind was so cloudy by then that he really had no concept of what was happening. Jim and I had been on our knees the previous night in the middle of our living room floor praying that God would mercifully take both of them home before morning so that we wouldn't have to do this terrible thing.

But God didn't take them, and my parents became homeless at the ages of eighty-one and ninety-four. It was the worst grief I have ever experienced in my life. I desperately wanted to take them both to my own home and care for them. However, at that point, Dad had full-blown Alzheimer's and Mother was not far behind mentally, and her physical condition was extreme. She had lost almost all motor ability.

I knew the futility of trying to care for them at home because my sister, Sylvia, and brother-in-law, Matt, had already tried it earlier, before our mother's condition had deteriorated so badly. They had taken Mother and Dad to stay with them at their home in Macon, Georgia. After only a few weeks, though, they had realized that our parents' needs were too great for home care—even with hired help to take the night shift. We brought them back to Florida and tried it ourselves for a few days, but after being up around the clock day after day, we knew we could not continue. That's when we started checking into assisted living facilities. The ALF we eventually chose seemed the best, and they talked of helping Mother get her strength back through physical therapy. We had high hopes.

After Mother's failed brain surgery, her condition deteriorated to the point where the State of Florida stepped in. On a routine visit to the ALF, an inspector for the State had pronounced Mother and Dad too debilitated for ALF supervision, had demanded that we secure around-the-clock, skilled nursing care, and had given us only forty-eight hours to move them from the ALF into an appropriate care arrangement. Although our folks had a respectable amount in savings, we had to consider how long it would last if drained by the extreme cost of *two* twenty-four-hour, private duty nurses. Two, because by that time Mother was a two-person lift. Even though she weighed only about a hundred pounds, her motor abilities were almost zero. She was unable to "help" with the lift at all, so it was like lifting a hundred pounds of dead weight. The situation seemed impossible, and I felt completely powerless to do anything except place my parents in a nursing home.

I have explained this decision in some detail here because I was one of those people who said that I would never, ever put someone I love in a nursing home. Yet I came to a point where I felt that I had no other choice. And I suspect that some of you reading this may have been placed into a position where you felt you had no choice—or if you haven't yet been in that position, you may be some time in the future. I want you to know that I beat up on myself for a long time. Even to this day I sometimes rehash it and ask myself why I couldn't have done better. I've had to learn that hindsight makes things look easier than they were.

In hindsight, I tell myself that I could have been a Superwoman instead of a mere human. I could have overcome anything. The truth is that given the same set of circumstances again, I would have been compelled to do the same thing. If one parent had been failing mentally and the other physically, perhaps I could have kept them at home. But with *both* parents failing mentally and physically, it was insurmountable, and I knew it. And now I have to learn to forgive myself for the crime of being human with limitations, and if you are in similar circumstances, you will have to learn to forgive yourself as well.

As we rode along in the handicap transport van that day, my mother weeping and Dad wondering aloud, my thoughts went back to the day I initially learned my widowed mother had a suitor. My mother had met my stepfather in the fall of 1987 more than three years after my daddy's death on January 1, 1984. My stepfather's first wife, Elmira, had passed away only a few months prior to his initially asking my mother for a date. Their first date was to a nondescript local restaurant for a cup of coffee one evening after choir practice. It sounds so "Mayberry RFD," doesn't it?

My sister and I and my soon-to-be stepsister and stepbrother and our spouses were all relieved that Mother and Dad had found each other right there in the small church they both attended. My stepsister and stepbrother would later describe to us how devastated Dad had been following Elmira's death and how he had "blossomed" again when he had been able to catch Mother's eye. My sister and I had been watching our mother grow increasingly depressed as the years passed after Daddy's death. Mother still held a full-time job as manager of the shoe department of a local department store, but she had no social life, other than church. And whenever she was home, she was in bed. She scheduled herself for the second shift at the store so she could sleep late and report to work around noon. Then, arriving home at about 9:30 at night, she would make something to eat—often nothing more than a bowl of cereal—and go to bed.

Not only were we worried about her psyche, we were also concerned for her safety. A man had broken into her unpretentious home late one evening as she lay in bed reading a book in her bedroom in the back part of the house. When she heard the noise at her front door, she bolted from her bedroom just in time to see the intruder opening the door and stepping into the living room. Screaming like a banshee, she literally scared "the devil" out of him, and he fled the house. Police found him later and described him as a drunk who was trying to sneak into what he mistakenly thought was his own home without waking his wife. It seemed harmless enough, and yet we couldn't help but wonder whether the story was true and worry that Mother might actually have been in serious peril.

My mother was one of the bravest people I have ever known. I had never known her to be afraid of anything. And I'm sure that in the heat of the moment, she was not the least bit afraid. In fact, I have always thought the intruder to have been exceedingly lucky that he had the presence of mind to flee. I can't imagine his fate if Mother had actually gotten hold of him!

It wasn't until later on, as Mother began to ruminate about the incident, that she became frightened. It was a fright from which she never truly recovered. As she became older and her mind began to fail, she would prop chairs under door handles and put obstacles in the pathway of the door before she and Dad retired at night. We became concerned that they would be unable to get out of the house in case of fire.

Mother and Dad had a short courtship and got married within a few months of their first date. Mother was sixty-eight at the time and Dad was eighty-one. He was a cancer survivor, having had surgery for colon cancer a year earlier. Mother had a lung disease that was finally diagnosed as a mycobacterial infection from a bacteria found in birds' feces. The doctor theorized that Mother had probably had the condition since childhood when she was raised on a farm that had a henhouse full of chickens, and the chore of gathering eggs from the henhouse often fell to Mother.

Apparently, the bacteria (similar to tuberculin) can be encapsulated in the body so that it does little or no harm until a later event compromises the immune system and the bacteria escapes the encapsulation. The doctor surmised that caring for our (biological) daddy during his last illness had sapped Mother's strength so that her immune system had weakened, and the disease had manifested.

Because of Dad's prior cancer history (and his age) and Mother's ongoing lung disease, we worried that they would face overwhelming health challenges and that they would not have many enjoyable years together.

We may have worried, but they didn't seem to. They were like teenagers in love. Both families watched in amusement as they started their new life together and carried on like young lovers. We called them "Romeo and Juliet." They had a wonderful romance. I prayed that God would give them some time together—and He did. He gave them almost fourteen years, and at least eleven of those years were really good. Then the health problems began in earnest.

Along with praying that the Lord would give Mother and Dad some vibrant years together, I also prayed that when the time came to call them home, He would be merciful and would take them quickly. I didn't want them to suffer as I had seen my daddy suffer. Knowing how much they were in love and how much they depended on each other, I knew that one would have an extremely difficult time dealing with the death of the other. I believe in a God of miracles, so I prayed in confidence. I asked that, when their times came, Mother and Dad would pass away quickly, and that they would go to heaven together or within a short time of each other so that the remaining one wouldn't experience prolonged grief.

Perhaps it was a childishly naive prayer for a woman of

my age. (I was fifty-eight when they died.) Regardless, I knew God to be loving, and I trusted that He would honor a pure and simple prayer that loved ones not suffer seemingly needless physical or emotional pain.

God let me down. He did—and I've had a hard time getting over it. Mother and Dad suffered untold misery. When they had their wits about them enough to understand, they hated the nursing home. When they didn't, they wandered around like lost children—Dad ambling along pushing Mother in her wheelchair, aimlessly going nowhere. It was heartbreaking to watch. Yet, I couldn't stay away. I went every day. The nursing supervisor spoke with me one day and suggested as gently as possible that my hovering might be making it more difficult for my parents to adjust. How does one adjust to having lost his or her home, mind and health? Does it help if one also feels abandoned?

There were many abandoned souls at that place. I seldom ever saw family members or friends visiting other patients. The nursing home held a regular monthly family conference. All families who had residents in the home received a notice of the conference each month. When I got my notice that first month, I immediately marked it on my calendar and showed up at the conference room at the appointed time. *No one was there.*

I asked at the nurses' station about the conference, and

I was met with a blank stare. Finally, one of the nurses said that she would page the activities director. He eventually showed up and hastily assembled some other staff members. I thought it was odd that no one had been there on time. Regardless, it was a good meeting. They carefully explained the care that was outlined for my parents, and I felt much better for having been given such complete information.

When the conference rolled around the next month, I arrived, and there was a replay of the scenario from the previous month. No staff member was there initially, someone had to be summoned, they hastily gathered together and met with me. This seemed so bizarre that I asked what was going on. Someone quietly explained that, while the conference was posted on the bulletin board and notices were mailed to all families, *no one ever showed up*. So the staff was completely unprepared when I sincerely showed an interest in my parents' care and actually arrived each month for the conference. I went to the meeting every month until Mother and Dad had both passed away. The assembly always consisted only of a few staff persons and me—the lone family member who showed up. I felt extreme sorrow for those sweet, lonely souls whose families never came. Perhaps it was just too painful to see the suffering. I can surely identify with that. But I *had* to go. I couldn't allow my mother and dad to feel abandoned. Weren't they suffering enough from all their other tremendous losses?

Because old scars have healed and a lot of forgiveness has taken place since our parents' deaths in 2001, I won't talk about the horrendous strain of family disputes during this time. But, trust me, it was extremely stressful. At one point I developed a case of stress-induced shingles. I've had friends and relatives who have had shingles, and they have described to me how extremely painful this disease is. My emotional pain was so intense, however, that I hardly noticed the added physical pain.

The trouble was that we all cared very much for our parents' welfare, but we had quite different ideas of what was best for them. Everyone seemed to be pulling in different directions, with very little communication. Looking back, I think we all now feel that we could have tried harder and communicated better. It was just an extremely difficult time, but our family survived it, we learned from it, and, thank God, we are closer today because of it, or maybe in spite of it. Shared, grievous experiences either draw families closer or blow them apart. The past several years have been a season of recovery for our family. Time has a way of healing, if we will allow it.

Dad passed away on August 26, 2001—two months before his ninety-fifth birthday. The previous week, he had returned to the nursing home after a short stay in the hospital following a heart attack. At that point, it had become necessary to put Mother and Dad in separate rooms because Mother was unable to comprehend that Dad could no longer get up countless times a night to help her. Bedridden and helpless, she desperately wanted Dad's help and the comfort of his strength, but her failing mind allowed her no insight into Dad's own disabilities.

I was at the nursing home on the day of his death, and he was well enough to eat part of his dinner early that evening. I did not expect that he would pass away that night. *He was all alone.* I felt terrible that no one was there with him. I painfully remember going to the nursing home the next morning to tell Mother that Dad had passed away during the night.

Jim and I got up early and went to the home so that Mother did not have to hear the news from someone else. I felt that she might take it better coming from us. Jim and I took our sad little journey in complete silence. When we arrived, we found Mother sitting in a special chair that would accommodate someone of her extreme disability and immobility. I can never erase from my mind the picture of her sitting there softly crying—all hope gone. Does anyone really know what it feels like to lose *all* hope? I think I experienced it with her. . .and it was *crushing*.

During the final years of her life, my mother and I had become very close in our spirits. We understood each other to a degree that I often felt I had the ability to experience her feelings right along with her. I felt her hopelessness and despair that awful day. It burned a hole in my spirit. It's been a stubborn hole that resists healing.

Two weeks and two days after Dad passed away, America was attacked by terrorists on September 11, 2001, and the World Trade Center was destroyed. We all watched in horror as the newscasts repeatedly replayed the chilling sights of the plane crashing into the second tower and the fall of both towers. It was surreal. We mourned as a nation, and I mourned the loss of my sweet stepfather and the loss of America's innocence. I wept when newscaster Dan Rather choked up as he stated that we can no longer sing the words to *American the Beautiful*:

> *Thine alabaster cities gleam,*
> *undimmed by human tears.*

On November 15, 2001, a mere eleven weeks after Dad's death, Mother passed away. Knowing that she was very near death, I had haunted the nursing home for the days and nights prior. At about midnight the night she died, I went home. I had been sitting by her bed for hours right by myself. I have to point out here that God let me go through most of the nursing home experience almost entirely alone. My husband, usually caring and empathetic, seemed practically oblivious to my emotional and spiritual pain and my complete exhaustion.

Family members came whenever possible, but my sister and her husband lived five hundred miles away, and he had heart disease. My stepsister and her husband lived an hour's drive away. She had suffered a stroke herself the previous year, at age fifty-five, and her husband had a serious heart condition. I believe her stroke had been brought on by the stress of dealing with our parents' decline. My stepbrother and his wife lived on the opposite coast of Florida, and he wasn't in good health either, having suffered some type of cardiovascular event a few months prior. My sons all lived in other states and were leading busy lives. So, more often than not, I sat alone at the nursing home by my mother's and previously by my stepfather's bedside. This night was no different.

Jim had stopped by earlier and then had gone home to get some sleep. Around midnight I decided that if I were going to be able to get through the following day of vigilance, I'd better go home and try to get some sleep as well. Mother appeared to be resting. I went home. The phone rang about three hours later. It was one of the night nurses telling me that Mother had passed away. I felt awful that she, too, had died *all alone*, just as Dad had.

God had honored my prayer that neither Mother nor Dad would linger long after the first one had passed away. But I felt betrayed that He had *not* granted my simple request that they be spared the agony of long, lingering illnesses and miserable deaths. I guess death is never pretty. But I'm always saddened—and yes, bitter—even now when I hear that "so-and-so passed away peacefully, surrounded by loved ones." Both Mother and Dad had died all alone. No loving family surrounded either of them. I was exhausted.

I cried. I cried for days, I cried for weeks, I cried for months. At one point, my husband said in concern, "Honey, I think you have gone beyond normal grief. I think you may need some professional help." He didn't understand that I wasn't mourning my parents' deaths. We are all terminal. We will all die. It's not an option. I knew they were going to die, and I knew that if things played out in a normal pattern, they would die before I did, and I would suffer the loss. I wasn't mourning their deaths so much as I was mourning the manner in which they died. And I was mourning the loss of my trust in God.

That's the spiritual vacuum I was in when I met the puppy whom we named Bandit. Through Bandit, I began to relearn God's love. I began to see God and His love through puppy eyes.

Chapter Three
Seeing God Through Puppy Eyes

Trust in the LORD with all your heart,
And lean not on your own understanding;
In all your ways acknowledge Him,
And He shall direct your paths *(away from fireants!)*
Proverbs 3:5-6 *(my slight revision!)*

As I watched the antics and learning experiences of my new puppy, I began to see the similarities between God's love for His children and my love for this little creature—not that human love could ever compare with the sheer enormity of God's love. But we are created in His image, and when we receive Christ, His Holy Spirit comes to live inside us. So we are like Him in image and in spirit. Perhaps it's not too great a leap, therefore, to come to an appreciation of certain aspects of God's love by examining our own love for one another and for other creatures—such as one truly adorable puppy!

Bandit turned out to be such a rascal that we ended up having to hire a trainer to help us deal with him. When one contemplates the need for a dog trainer, images of Dobermans, Rottweilers, German Shepherds and other large breeds immediately come to mind. One doesn't generally think of a Shih Tzu puppy hardly bigger than a teacup. But we had one little renegade on our hands! He didn't like the leash and fought it. He "raped" his teddy bear and other stuffed toys. We endured several bites—some playful, some not so playful. Razor sharp puppy teeth can do some real damage—even if the bite is playful.

Bandit lived up to his name! He was truly a bandit and a scalawag!

Not all of his behavior was delinquent; however, some of it was simply spirited exuberance that needed to be channeled into more appropriate and socially-acceptable behavior. Almost immediately we asked the trainer about Bandit's "raping" of his toys and learned that we had a very "alpha" puppy, and that this disconcertingly sexual act was a way of expressing dominance.

Although Bandit resisted training—and anything else that wasn't his own way—we knew that we had to curb some of his excesses. He had to learn what a quick jerk on the leash means. He had to learn to behave. He needed the "Ten Commandments" of good dog behavior. He rebelled against training, but he soon learned that there are wills stronger than his.

Three hundred dollars and many sessions later, what Bandit really "got" from the training was "stay." He can *stay* with the best of them! But don't ask him to come. He has no idea what "come" means. His trainer had explained to me that we needed to communicate with Bandit in one-word commands because he wouldn't be able to understand phrases. I beg to differ. Bandit understood the eleven-word phrase, "Do you want to go for a ride in the car?" the second time he heard it. And he bounded joyfully toward the garage and leapt with delight into the awaiting car. Yet no matter how many times it's been demonstrated to him that he is to come to the person is calling "come," he appears to have never quite understood that word and pays the caller no attention whatsoever.

As I worked with Bandit, I began to understand more and more about my relationship with God and about how He watches over me, and every detail of my life. Fire ants are a good example. Bandit got into fire ants a couple of times and suffered rather severe repercussions both times. He tends toward reactions. He reacted to a puppy vaccination so severely that he almost died.

I had taken Bandit, then about ten weeks old, to the vet for the last of his "puppy shots" and a rabies vaccination. I'm not in favor of inoculations, and I had discussed this previously with the vet. He had been my veterinarian for almost all the fourteen years of my previous dog's life. Charlie had been a regular at his clinic. I trust this doctor implicitly, but as I have become more in tune with natural treatments and diet, I am less convinced that vaccinations are actually a good thing. The doctor persuaded me to continue Bandit's inoculations at least through his initial "puppy shots." The breeder had begun the series while Bandit was still in her care. My vet reasoned that these preliminary immunizations would provide Bandit a measure of protection during his early and more vulnerable years. I trusted the doctor's judgment. And, of course, the rabies inoculation isn't optional, since it's required by law.

Bandit got his rabies shot and the last round of his puppy shots around five o'clock on a Friday afternoon. Some unsolicited advice here: Do not get inoculations or other potentially problematic procedures late on a Friday afternoon. Chances are you could end up, as we did, at an expensive emergency veterinary clinic.

Initially, Bandit seemed fine. He was quiet and slept a lot, but that was normal in his early weeks of life. Around 9:30 that evening, however, it occurred to me that I hadn't seen him for a while, and I started looking for him. I found him collapsed on the kitchen floor, his face distended, his eyes swollen almost shut. He was completely lethargic, and he yelped painfully as I attempted to pick him up.

I screamed for Jim, and he came running into the kitchen. "Quick!" I said. "We have to get Bandit to the doctor!"

One look at our puffy pet convinced Jim that I was right. I carefully picked Bandit up and wrapped him lightly in a towel, trying my best not to cause him additional pain. Apparently, any movement brought pain to his ballooning body. We jumped into our van with him and raced to the emergency animal clinic in Sarasota—about twenty miles from our home. Bandit weighed no more than two or three pounds at the time. He was so small and extremely ill. I was terrified that he was going to die. I prayed silently and then turned to look at Jim with tears streaming down my face.

"I don't think I can take another loss of someone I love right now," I grieved. Jim was well aware of how fragile I was emotionally. It had been a little over a year since the deaths of my mother and stepfather. Jim had been greatly concerned over my intense grief during the past year. I think he knew in the depths of his being that my heart couldn't take another death. And, you know what? God knew it, too. God heard my frantic cry for help as we sped down the dark Interstate—racing against time, praying we would get to medical help in time to save this baby dog.

When we arrived, someone immediately took Bandit from my arms and carried him into a treatment room behind a closed door. I have always gone right into the treatment room whenever I have taken a pet for a vet visit. So I was shocked when a clinician took Bandit from me and closed the door. I think she expected the worst. Apparently, she thought the little fellow might not make it, and she didn't want me to be on hand for that awful moment when he breathed his last.

Within a relatively short while—but what seemed like an eternity—the door opened, and the doctor smiled at me. It was one of the most welcome smiles I have ever seen! She had given Bandit a shot of Benadryl and Prednisone, and he came around quickly. This may sound like a sacrilege, but I feel certain that the companions (in Mark 2:1-12) who let the paralytic down through a roof on a pallet at Jesus' feet, felt no more elation at the friend's miraculous healing than I felt at that moment! I felt that God had indeed performed a miracle in giving my sweet little friend back to me from the brink of death.

Only a month or so after that terrifying night, Bandit got into fire ants while we were out for a walk early one evening. He started having labored breathing as I picked the ants from him, and his face began to swell. The doctor at the emergency clinic had advised me to always keep children's Benadryl on hand, so thankfully I was prepared and gave Bandit a dose immediately. Again, we jumped into the van and headed for the clinic. Have you ever noticed that emergencies with children or pets never, ever occur when the pediatrician's office or the veterinarian's office is open? The emergency animal clinic is quite expensive, and we were dreading the cost as we again sped along the Interstate. By the time we arrived, the Benadryl had started to work, and Bandit seemed almost normal. Jim, ever mindful of fiscal economy, was in favor of heading back home. I wasn't so sure.

We ended up hanging around on the parking lot for about a half hour just to verify that Bandit was okay. He seemed fine as he walked around sniffing the grass and bushes in the flower beds near the pavement. Finally, we decided that he was going to be okay, and we went home.

So I watch carefully for fire ants, and I keep the Benadryl handy. Since we live in Florida, there are fire ant mounds in abundance. When we are out walking and Bandit is having a wonderful time bouncing along the roadway, he doesn't understand when I pull up on the leash and drag him away from the direction he is headed. I see the fire ant mound. He does not.

I think that's when I first starting comparing God's care of me with my care of Bandit. I could see the danger of the direction Bandit was headed, and I pulled him away. He didn't like being pulled away, and he chafed at the leash and halter. But my guiding, loving hand would not let him continue in the direction he was headed—because it meant certain disaster.

How many times have my plans been derailed and I haven't understood why? It occurred to me, in observing Bandit pulling on the leash, that I haven't understood because I am not

God. Just as Bandit doesn't understand that there are fire ants ahead—and he never will understand it—I haven't understood what it is that God is pulling me back from.

I need to learn that when my plans are countermined, it's for my own good. That takes trust, because—like Bandit—I don't even know the danger *exists*, much less what the danger *is*. And, I have to come to terms with the fact that I may *never* know. Bandit will never know that those ants are there. His little doggy mind has no concept of fire ants. Even when he was covered in them, he had no idea why his skin was smarting. As I was frantically grabbing ants off him (and was getting stung myself), he mistakenly thought that somehow I had something to do with his pain. Needless to say, he was getting pretty upset with me.

Now isn't that just like most of us? God is mercifully in the process of rescuing us from something we have gotten ourselves into, and we lash out at Him—thinking that He is somehow responsible for our pain.

Bandit was trying his best to understand why he was getting stung and to do something about his predicament. So, besides biting at me, he was also biting at the multitude of ants on his body. No doubt, this merely resulted in his getting stung on his mouth as well. What was obvious to me, but not to Bandit, was that he couldn't rescue himself. In fact, all his efforts were merely compounding the problem. He actually was hindering me from effectively delivering him from the fire ants. It occurs to me that we do the same thing. We try our utmost to fix a situation that only God can fix and many times our efforts only compound the problem and hinder God's deliverance.

God has given us a perfect guide book—His infallible word. And He has given us His inexhaustible love. We can rest in both. When troubles mount up and seem to overwhelm us, we can cease our frantic efforts and merely be still and know that He is God. He is the God of our circumstances, and He is the "fix" for our troubles. As we still our minds and hearts and stop flailing about, God can perform the rescue that only He can do. And in case you are wondering, I don't have this wired either. I continue to flail and bite at the fire ants in my life instead of just resting in God. But I'm learning. I *am* learning.

In Ken Gire's excellent book *Windows of the Soul*,[1] he compares the stillness of the soul to the stillness of the axis of a wheel. He points out how the motionless axis gives stability, and without it, the wheel would fly off or bind up. If we quiet our spirits, like an axis, we can rest in our Father's omnipotent ability to quiet all the circumstances that are whirling around us or to use the circumstances to move us in the right direction. We can be still, and He *will* deliver us. *Be still and know that I am God*, Psalm 46:10 (KJV).

As I have continued to guide Bandit away from fire ants and other dangers through hard pulls on his leash, I have come to compare the leash with God's word. His word is a comfort as well as a guide for our lives. It's a boundary that gives us solace and security. When we remain inside the confines of God's word, we have the sense that all is right with our world. When we are outside His word and trying to run our own show, we feel insecure.

Bandit isn't particularly comfortable outside without his leash. I have taught him to go into our back yard unleashed for a quick "pee-pee." I let him out the back door and stand watch over him until he finishes his job. As soon as he is done, he bounds back toward me, and we go inside. A couple of times, however, he has had a sudden impulse to race over into the neighbor's yard. I've found that the best thing I can do in that instance is run as hard as I can in the *opposite* direction. I make a beeline for our door, and Bandit makes a beeline for me. With no leash to give him security and with me rapidly retreating from his view, he feels a sudden and overpowering insecurity and runs after me.

When I am feeling insecure or struggling with a weighty decision, I find that I do best when I make a beeline for God, running to Him in prayer and seeking guidance from His word. I am thankful for God's word as a sure and constant guide. I feel the security of His word, just as Bandit feels the security of the leash. Without it, life would be unbearably frightening.

Thy word is a lamp unto my feet and a light unto my path
Psalm 119:105

Thy rod and thy staff they comfort me.
Psalm 23:4b

Chapter Four
Taming the 2-lb. Beast

The Lord is near to those who have a broken heart,
And saves such as have a contrite spirit.
Psalm 34:18

If we confess our sins,
he is faithful and just to forgive us our sins,
and to cleanse us from all unrighteousness.
I John 1:9 (KJV)

But when he was still a great way off,
his father saw him and had compassion,
and ran and fell on his neck and kissed him
And the son said to him,
"Father, I have sinned against heaven and in your sight,
and am no longer worthy to be called your son."
But the father said to his servants,
"Bring out the best robe and put it on him,
and put a ring on his hand and sandals on his feet.
And bring the fatted calf here and kill it,
and let us eat and be merry;
for this my son was dead and is alive again;
he was lost and is found."
Luke 15:20b-24a

We got off to a rough start with Bandit. He was disarmingly cute and adorable. It was hard to imagine that he could be anything but sweet. He wasn't. Bandit is a very "alpha" male dog. He just happens to be a pint-sized one.

Our first task was finding a name for him. I've never been very good at naming pets. My first dog was named "Flappy." He was a border collie mix whose ears flapped when he ran. I've never been much more imaginative than that when naming pets. We have friends who have a black and white Shih Tzu named Oreo. And we have friends whose Lhasa Apso is named Monte. How classy! I'm impressed that anyone could come up with such creative names. But I'm always at a loss when it comes to names—and not just for pets. My first child was on earth almost a week before I came up with a name for him! Okay, give me a break. He was six weeks premature. I wasn't prepared, and I was young—only twenty-one.

As we pondered over a name for our diminutive new boarder, Jim suddenly declared, "Well, you know he looks like a bandit—with his little mask." The little fellow has great black circles around his eyes, and the circles extend on the sides of his face back toward his ears, looking indeed like a bandit's mask. Since Jim had not been thrilled about getting a dog, I thought it would be a really special thing for him to choose the name. So, "Bandit" it was.

Our first night with Bandit was typical for a new puppy

taken away from his mother and siblings. He cried as if his tiny heart would break, and I felt so sorry for him. I ended up sitting in a recliner all night trying to catch some sleep and holding Bandit close so that, hopefully, he wouldn't feel forsaken, and he could take comfort from the warmth of my body against his.

I was reminded of the many times in my life when my Heavenly Father has held me the same way—times when I felt so lonely I thought I would die. And I have felt the warmth of His great presence in the midst of my misery. *God is our refuge and strength a very present help in trouble.* Psalm 46:1.

And so passed the first night for Bandit in his new home.

The day went fairly well. We played with him, and I took him outside every nanosecond to make sure he learned that the yard was the place to do his "peeps" and "poops." I opted not to paper train him. I wanted to make sure that he never got any notion that it was ever okay to do his business in the house. Therefore, I was quite diligent in seeing to it that he went outside regularly. It was like having a new baby in the house. It seemed as though I was up all night not only taking Bandit outside every two or three hours but also tending to him as he wailed over the loss of his doggy family. By the dawn of the third day, I was exhausted. So I asked the advice of my friend, Carol, who has been a dog groomer for at least a quarter of a century. She suggested that I place Bandit in a cardboard box by my bed, and when he fretted, drop my hand over the side of the bed and into his box and stroke him to give him reassurance as he adjusted to life in his new family and without the only family he had ever known in his short eight weeks of existence.

On the fourth night, we had a defining moment. I was sitting in the recliner holding Bandit up against my neck—our usual pose in the evening hours before bedtime. I decided that I should probably take him outside, since it had been a couple of hours since his last visit to the grass. Bandit, I soon discovered, had other ideas. I don't know if he simply didn't want to go out or if he had decided to show me who was boss once and for all, but as I walked out the door with him holding him close to my neck, he suddenly growled and lunged toward my face. He bit me soundly on the mouth. His razor-sharp puppy teeth tore through my lips and opened a wound that gushed blood all down my shirt. I was stunned! How could this cute little ball of fluff that I had loved and cared for so carefully for the past three days and nights—with hardly any sleep or any relief—how could he turn on me and bite me? This wasn't a puppy nip. He meant business! My lips quickly swelled as I held my head over the bathroom sink, blood dripping onto the white porcelain. I was heartbroken. And, I was mad!

I started to have extreme misgivings about having acquired this puppy. I wondered if he were somewhat deranged—perhaps the product of a bad gene in the Shih Tzu pool. But, mostly, I just felt betrayed and bewildered. I had fallen so in love with this little guy. I thought he loved me, too. How could he turn on me like that?

Only a few nights later I happened to see a short segment on the evening news where one of the reporters complained of having received a severe bite on his ear dealt by his new puppy. He talked about how shocking he thought this behavior was at first, but then he spoke with an animal trainer who explained that, after all, he had a wild creature who was in the taming process. I felt a little better about the episode with Bandit. Apparently, getting a sharp bite from a new puppy wasn't something that far out of the ordinary.

That night, however, I had no such conciliatory thoughts. I scolded Bandit and put him in a small cage that we had bought for him when he first came home with us. I had heretofore been too indulgent to put him in it. It was a green hard plastic "condo" with a grate-type door that latched. I dumped Bandit unceremoniously into the cage and left him to ponder his great transgression. He didn't ponder at all; he promptly went to sleep. He knew he was in deep trouble, and in typical male fashion, he opted for "avoidance sleep."

I put ice on my swollen lips and cried. I cried from pain in my lips and from pain in my heart. I loved the little boy, and he had turned on me. I contemplated what to do. Should I take Bandit back to the breeder and tell her she had sold me a wild dog? After an hour or so, I went to bed—lips swollen and eyes swollen from crying. I was a mess!

I was awakened a couple of hours later by the sound of the most pitiful puppy cries I had ever heard. I let him cry! He was a mean, hateful Gremlin. He looked all cute and fluffy, but inside a demon resided that came at you with sharp, menacing teeth! I was going to let him stew in his misery. As I lay there listening to his distress, his cries became more intense. He was getting into some serious bawling now. Still I waited. I wasn't sure I wanted to open that cage door or put my hand in there. I wasn't ready to sacrifice another body part!

Finally, I could stand his pitiful cries no longer. I got up and walked into the darkened kitchen where Bandit's cage was. He wailed as if the loneliness of the entire world was upon him. As he sensed my approach, his squalling went into high gear. I gingerly opened the cage door and stepped back not knowing what kind of monster would charge forth. Instead of charging, Bandit gathered his little self close to my feet. He literally hugged my feet and cried as if his tiny heart would break. He shook, he sniffled, he cried. He shook like a child who has cried to the point of exhaustion so that all he can do is inhale great gulps of air and then shudder with each exhale. I have never seen a more sincere demonstration of true repentance.

My heart melted.

I picked him up and held him close—still not entirely

sure he wouldn't turn from Jekyll to Hyde at any moment. He snuggled against me. In his puppy way, he begged for forgiveness. And, of course, I forgave him on the spot. I carried him outside to take care of his business—after all, it had been at least three hours since I last attempted to take him out. And then I took him into our bed. I couldn't think of anything else to do with him. I couldn't put him back into the cage. I couldn't bear to hear his wretched cries again. I desperately needed to sleep. (The box-by-the-bed idea had failed miserably.) And, I needed to take him outside again in two or three hours. Putting him in our bed seemed to be the only solution. And that's where he sleeps to this day—in our bed between Jim and me.

Every night—since that first time—he gets into bed, rummages around a bit and then settles himself right by my neck. As his little body relaxes, he sighs a deep, puppy sigh. All is well; he is where he belongs; he is loved; everything is right in his world. That's the feeling I had yearned to rediscover in my relationship with my Heavenly Father. Maybe this little creature could teach me how to do that.

I have birthed and raised two sons, and I have a wonderful stepson who came into my life when he was only eight years old. We have never allowed a child into our bed. It was just something we never started—because (as we have so aptly proven with Bandit), it's extremely difficult to stop. Once they worm their way into the bed, you just can't get them out again.

Obviously, the point of this story is forgiveness. Forgiving Bandit reminded me of all the times I have lashed out at God and of all the times He has picked me up and held me again when I came to Him in repentance. When I forgave Bandit and not only took him back but gave him a more exalted position than his previous state, I suddenly caught a glimpse of God's grace. A glimpse of how He loves no matter what. You have to admit that biting the face of someone who loves you is a pretty egregious sin. Yet, of how many and much more egregious sins has God forgiven me? Of how many sins and how egregious ones has He forgiven you?

I think of the parable of the prodigal son in Luke 15:11-32. After "wasting his substance on riotous living" (as the *King James Version* poetically puts it*)* in a distant land, the son came to his senses and went home to his father. And his father, seeing him away off in the distance, *ran* to meet him. I think of the lyrics to the popular Christian song *When God Ran*[2] by Benny Hester and John Parenti:

> *Almighty God, the great I Am*
> *Immovable rock, omnipotent, powerful,*
> *awesome Lord*
> *Victorious warrior,*
> *commanding King of Kings*
> *Mighty conqueror;*
> *and the only time,*

> *the only time I ever saw Him run*
>
> *Was when He ran to me, He took me in His arms*
> *Held my head to His chest, said*
> *"My son's come home again"*
> *Lifted my face, wiped the tears from my eyes*
> *With forgiveness in His voice He said,*
> *"Son, do you know I still love you?"*
> *He caught me by surprise when God ran.*

Yes, the son was repentant. But his Father didn't even wait to see if he was repentant—he just ran toward the son who once was lost but now was found. He greeted him, he embraced him, he kissed him, he put a robe on him and shoes on him and threw a party for him—exalting him. Why? Because he came *HOME!* He came home to the Father's love, and love never fails! (I Corinthians 13:8).

Dear friend, has God's love ever failed you? Really? Has His love really ever failed you? There have been times in my life when I have thought so. But once I have gotten some perspective on God's supposed "failing," I have seen that He never defaulted. But I didn't yet have such a perspective on what seemed to be God's betrayal when my mother and stepfather suffered so and died—and I knew I might not ever understand.

But this one thing I know. The most profound and meaningful lessons I have learned in life have been learned through pain and suffering—both physical and emotional. It is sometimes difficult to connect the dots from our pain to God's love. Yet, this experience with Bandit, began to open my eyes to how powerful love is and what a wonderful promise we have that love never, ever fails!

> He who does not love does not know God
> for *God is love*. [Emphasis mine.]
> I John 4:8

> Love never fails.
> I Corinthians 13:8a

Chapter Five
Providing for Bandit's Special Needs

Therefore do not worry, saying, "What shall we eat?"
or "What shall we drink?" or "What shall we wear?" . . .
For your heavenly Father knows that you need all these things.

But seek first the kingdom of God and His righteousness,
and all these things shall be added to you.
Matthew 6:31-33

It soon became apparent that Bandit had a delicate digestive system. Translation: There was no dog food on the planet that would not cause him diarrhea and/or bouts of vomiting. What to do? I finally started preparing his food myself. I cooked fresh chicken, tore it off the bones and prepared brown rice in the chicken broth. I added lots of garlic (to repel fleas) and a few veggies as I cooked the rice, so that Bandit's diet, hopefully, would contain a complement of vitamins and minerals, protein and carbohydrates. To be on the safe side, I crushed a chlorella tablet (green, nutrient-loaded algae) and added it to his food just before he ate it, and I squirted omega-3 fish oils over it to keep his coat nice and shiny and help prevent any itchy skin issues. (Unwanted side effect: *Terrible* fish-breath!)

Bandit seemed to thrive on his diet for a while but then started having infrequent bouts of diarrhea and occasional vomiting. Then we moved into a new house, and he developed itchy skin. I wondered if the itching were environmental, since almost everyone in our new neighborhood had their yards chemically treated. I watched in dismay as Bandit continued to scratch himself more every day. I searched him for fleas and found none.

Finally, I took him to a holistic veterinarian. She agreed that the itching could be environment related but thought we should try different food, since itching is usually related to diet. She explained that with canines, the most likely dietary culprit is grain—but usually brown rice is innocuous. The usual culprits are wheat and corn. Regardless, she thought that Bandit might have developed an allergy to a steady diet of chicken and brown rice. Perhaps his system required more variety. After trying a number of different approaches, I finally asked myself what God had intended this diminutive carnivore to eat. The answer, of course, was raw meat—preferably fresh killed.

Well, I'm not a hunter, so Bandit had to settle for a raw meat preparation in frozen packs from the holistic dog food store. In case you are wondering, it "ain't cheap." But it works. Bandit improved tremendously—and for the first time in his life (literally!) he had normal "poop." I can't even begin to tell you how much we have endured dealing with Bandit's bouts of diarrhea—sometimes to the point of really watery, bloody—oh, well, you get the picture! Thankfully, Bandit never, ever poops in the house! But I have made a number of emergency vet visits because of concern that the poor little fellow was becoming dehydrated from persistent diarrhea.

The raw food worked like a charm. Getting Bandit accustomed to it was another matter. It took a long time to change him over to "raw." One caveat here: I'm not a veterinarian, and I'm not offering dietary advice for your pet. I'm only describing what worked for Bandit. Before you change anything about your own pet's diet, be sure you consult a veterinarian who thoroughly understands raw diet and your pet's particular condition, age and health issues.

What I eventually did, on the advice of a homeopathic veterinarian, was switch Bandit to raw meat—right from the grocery store. He took to it immediately. Apparently, he didn't object to raw meat at all, just to the expensive concoction I had been buying at the pet supply store. I add a small amount of raw ground up veggies, a pinch of raw minced garlic, green algae, omega-3 fatty acids, and the liquid stress formula that I was intending to market to the breeder the day I first met Bandit.

(She never did purchase any, by the way.) And, happily, I discovered that I could get the omega-3s in a blend consisting mostly of ground flax seed. No more fish breath!

The itching is gone. And to this day, I have found only about a half dozen fleas on Bandit in his entire life. He gets no flea repellant chemicals or medicines; he is naturally without fleas. Since parasites prey on the weak, a healthy dog is usually a parasite-free dog. Bandit is eating the raw food God intended a dog to eat. As in every aspect of life, following God's plan is the perfect way to health—spiritual and physical. Besides being much more healthful, the diet is actually quite inexpensive. It costs me considerably less than packaged or canned dog food. As a corollary, following God's plan in our lives invariably costs us much less in physical and mental anguish than going our own way.

Bandit watches me intently as I prepare his food. I put the prepared mixture of individual meal-sized portions in Ziplock bags and keep them in the freezer. I keep a couple of days' worth of food thawed ahead in the refrigerator.

It's a lot more work than opening a can of dog food or scooping some dry kibble from a bag. My reward is that I have a healthy dog who doesn't suffer from all the allergies and other aliments that plague most dogs raised on food that is roughly equivalent to the typical American diet—the diet that is killing typical Americans!

Do you think it ever crosses Bandit's doggy mind that I might not feed him on any given day? Do you think he worries about how much work I put into his diet, or that I might tire of it, or not be there for him? Does he worry that, when it's time to go out, I won't be there to "clothe" him in his halter, put his leash on him and go with him? I can't help but contrast Bandit's complete trust in me with my lack of trust in God.

In recent years, my husband and I had fancied ourselves to be real estate entrepreneurs. We had bought and sold a couple of "investment" houses and had made a good return on the investment. The idea was to buy a neglected house at a low price, quickly make any needed repairs and do some cosmetic upgrades, then sell it immediately before mortgage payments, insurance, taxes and other ongoing costs eroded any potential profit. Unfortunately, about two years ago, at the height of the real estate boom in Florida, we decided to buy two houses at once. Actually, I decided to do so, and Jim reluctantly went along with me. We closed on both of the houses the last day of September, 2005, and the real estate market in Florida died an instant death in October. Timing is everything!

We finally sold one of the houses nine months later, in June 2006, having invested a tremendous amount of money into remodeling. The second house finally sold in October of 2006—over a year from the date we had originally purchased it—and also after extensive (and expensive) remodeling. I don't think I need to detail the vast amount of expense we incurred and the emotional and financial strain of paying mortgages, taxes, insurance and maintenance on those two houses plus our own home. Both houses sold at tremendous losses. As a result, we are now forced to sell our own home. It was an extremely stressful, *educational* year.

I have awakened many a morning in a blind panic, wondering if we were going to end up out on the street—among the homeless. I have watched, with shame and heartache, as the inheritances our parents left us have been devoured by all the expenses of maintaining three houses. I am sometimes paralyzed with fear for the future. In the meanwhile, Bandit has remained confident that I will continue to feed him and take care of his every need.

So why have I doubted that my Heavenly Father will take care of me at least as well as I take care of my dog? Am I not much more to Him than a dog? I can hear echoing in my head, and down the corridors of time, the Savior's words, "O you of little faith."

> *Therefore I say to you, do not worry about your life,*
> *what you will eat or what you will drink;*
> *nor about your body, what you will put on.*
> *Is not life more than food and the body more than clothing?*
>
> *Look at the birds of the air,*
> *for they neither sow nor reap nor gather into barns;*
> *yet your heavenly Father feeds them.*

Are you not of more value than they?

Which of you by worrying can add one cubit to his stature?
So why do you worry about clothing?
Consider the lilies of the field, how they grow:
they neither toil nor spin;
and yet I say to you that even Solomon in all his glory
was not arrayed like one of these.

Now if God so clothes the grass of the field,
which today is, and tomorrow is thrown into the oven,
will He not much more clothe you, O you of little faith?

Therefore do not worry, saying, "What shall we eat?"
or "What shall we drink?" or
"What shall we wear?" . . . For your heavenly Father
knows that you need all these things.

But seek first the kingdom of God and His righteousness,
and all these things shall be added to you.
Matthew 6:25-33

Chapter Six
Bandit: The Tasmanian Devil

He has brought me to his banqueting house
and his banner over me was love.
Song of Solomon 2:4

I'm standing in the kitchen and Bandit is at my feet looking up at me with that sweet, innocent—well, seemingly sweet and innocent—face. I'm chatting him up, telling him that he's my "sweet Bandit boy," when it occurs to me that actually he sometimes isn't all that sweet. Bandit has two basic moods—Tasmanian Devil and catatonic. Shih Tzus are known for their loving natures—it's just that no one warned me about the flip side. When Bandit is in his Tasmanian Devil mood, he races wildly around the house, grabs one of his toys and shakes it ferociously—growling all the while. Or he engages in one of his favorite activities—nipping at my feet! He will run around and around me taking "love bites" at my feet while growling and barking gleefully. He zooms madly away at warp speed and

54

then dashes back, circles my feet, nipping and growling, inviting me to chase him as he speeds away again. If I join in the chase, it gets more frenzied. He means me no harm; he's just having a marvelous time—at my expense.

So, as I'm chatting him up on what a sweet boy he is, it occurs to me that in actuality he's a little hellion. And I tell him so. Then I realize that I'm often a hellion myself. I storm around trying to get my own way, ranting and raving when things aren't working out the way I think they should. I fly into rages, growling all the while and maybe even taking nips at the feet of the Master of the Universe. All very presumptuous of me, by the way—just as Bandit presumes on my good graces. He knows without a doubt that I adore him in spite of himself, and that I will work all things to his good—even if at times he doesn't think it's for his good at all—just as our Father promised us in Romans 8:28 that He will work *all* things together for good. We may not see the good at the time, but we have His promise. And His word is true. We can count on it.

Then I go into my other mood—just as Bandit does—when all I want is to be held and to relax in God's care. So I climb into my Father's lap and lie still (catatonic even) and gratefully receive the security of His steadfast love. Likewise, Bandit relishes climbing into my lap just to be held. When Bandit is in his affectionate mood, he will crawl up into my lap, settle himself down, sigh deeply, and rest contentedly in the protection of my arms. Sometimes I hold him like a baby, with him lying on his back cradled in my arms. He will go into an almost catatonic state. I stroke his ears, massage his toes, kiss his nose and face, rub his tummy and back. He has no concerns. He just basks in the security of knowing, without a doubt, that he is immeasurably loved.

Isn't that where we all long to be with our Creator? Isn't that why we all have a "God-sized" hole in our souls? Our Father created us to love Him and to receive His love. Our souls crave it. That's why it's such a rapturous experience when we actually feel His love enveloping us like a warm, cozy, favorite blanket. Then we know we are truly where we belong, and we feel secure and cherished.

The trainer said that I have made all the typical mistakes. That I have treated Bandit like a person, rather than as a dog. He said that I do the characteristic "womanly" thing of holding the dog and loving on him and treating him like a baby. He said that we would never get satisfactory training results as long as I acted this way. And you know what I thought? "So what!" That's what I thought. I have a dog because I want to love him and feel his love coming back to me. I don't want a little creature to order around and make me feel superior. I want to hold him, play with him, love on him—in other words, I want to enjoy his fellowship. It occurs to me that just maybe God feels the same way about me. *Yeah.*

True, it's a joy when Bandit does happen to actually obey me. He really does *stay* very well. If you could see him do it, you would know why I am so proud of him. And, I believe that God is pleased when one of His children actually obeys. But He doesn't stop loving us simply because we aren't the best at obeying. I love Bandit because I love him. I have no other reason. I love him just because he *is*. He doesn't have to prove himself to me. He merely has to *be*. And that's enough.

Okay, so I may never be able to enter him in a dog show. I may never be able to have friends over and show them what wonderful tricks my dog can do. That's fine. I didn't get a dog for those reasons. I got a dog to *love*. I am amazed with the knowledge that God feels the same way about me. It would be great if He could single me out as a shining example of obedience, as He said of Job in Job 1:8:

> *Have you considered My servant Job, that there is none like him on the earth, a blameless and upright man, one who fears God and shuns evil?*

It's highly unlikely that (in my wildest dreams) God would ever be able to give me such a compliment. But I am content in knowing that, though I may never be a model of obedience, God picked me out of the slave market of sin simply to *love* me.

Isn't that awesome?

57

Chapter Seven
Sleeping Secure in His Love

He gives His beloved sleep. Psalm 121:4b

He will rejoice over you with gladness,
He will quiet you with His love,
He will rejoice over you with singing.
Zephaniah 3:17

I think it's some sort of "hormonal thing" (isn't *everything* when we reach a certain age?), but in recent years, I seem to have lost something in my neurological makeup that produces sleep. And even on those nights when I'm able to drop off relatively easily, I often rouse at around three in the morning wide awake again. So I've come to a real appreciation of what a blessing a good night's sleep is! Those nights when I actually rest well and arise refreshed are really prized these days.

Bandit, on the other hand, sleeps a lot. He sleeps in my chair, he sleeps on the couch, he sleeps on the floor under the coffee table, he sleeps *on* the coffee table, he sleeps by me when

I work at the computer, he sleeps on the bathroom floor when I'm taking my shower and getting dressed, he sleeps all night every night in bed with Jim and me. He rests because he has no worries. He is secure. He knows he is loved. He knows his needs will be met.

I am sitting in my recliner one evening. Bandit has crawled up on the coffee table in front of me in the family room, and he is fast asleep. He looks so sweet when he is asleep. I just want so much to hold him. So I get up, slide him off the coffee table and into my waiting arms. I lie back in the recliner and stretch Bandit's little inert body on mine, and I stroke his fur and talk "love talk" to him—sweet, affectionate words as to a little child.

It's then that I remember the words from Psalm 127:2 that our Father *gives His beloved sleep*. I begin to ponder this verse as I sit stroking my napping dog. And it occurs to me that maybe God does the same to me when I'm asleep. It's a time when I am quiet—and maybe, like Bandit, I look sweet (well, maybe not, but He loves me anyway). I have absolutely no scriptural basis for this, but I imagine that He holds me, strokes my back, runs His divine fingers through my hair and talks "love talk" to me—his slumbering (sixty-three-year-old!) child. Then I remember the Psalm. God grants sleep to those He *loves!* Of course, He does. He does it so that He can love on them.

We live busy lives. The busyness keeps us almost frantic during our waking hours. Our Father God awaits our hours of repose so that we are quiet enough that He can love on us. He even *gives* us the sleep in the first place. Isn't that cool? He grants sleep to those He loves so that He has the opportunity to just pour out love on them.

> *Oh, dear Father, please grant me a good night's sleep tonight, and please use the opportunity to really love on me. I need your love, Father. I need to feel your unfathomable, unfailing, unchanging, unconditional love.*

I'm looking back over this chapter today, and I'm thinking about my mother being in a coma shortly before she died. Some of you may have a loved one in critical condition or in a coma right now, and you may be struggling to deal with it. Perhaps it will help to think about the Lord of Heaven and earth whispering words of love into the ear of your "sleeping" beloved. I have wept bitter tears because my mother died all alone in a nursing home. I truly believe that the Lord brought Mother to mind today as I reviewed this chapter. I think He wanted me to know that she most definitely was not alone. Up until her last few months on earth, my mother had always led a very active life. She was continually busy with something—work, children, grandchildren, cooking, cleaning, looking after my father, and later on my stepfather. She was never still for very long.

Perhaps, just perhaps, the Lord had some things He wanted to say to her to prepare her for the journey before He took her home, and perhaps the only way He could keep her attention long enough to do so was if she were asleep. If you have a loved one in such a state, perhaps the Lord has things to say to him or her as well. Look back at the beginning of this chapter and read again Zephaniah 3:17 and know that He rejoices over your loved one with gladness, quiets your beloved with His love, and then He rejoices over your darling with singing. We read that verse at my mother's funeral, and we played the song *When the Night is Falling*,[3] based on that scripture, and written and sung by Dennis Jernigan.

> *When the night is falling,*
> *and the day is done,*
> *I can hear You calling, "Come."*
> *I will come,*
> *While You sing over me.*
>
> *When the night surrounds me,*
> *all my dreams undone,*
> *I can hear You calling, "Come."*
> *I will come,*
> *While You sing over me.*
>
> *When the night would hide my way,*
> *I will listen until I hear you say:*
> *"How I love you, child, I love you.*
> *"How I love you, child, I love you.*
> *"How I love you!"*

Chapter Eight
Learning Love's Language

Come to Me all you who labor and are heavy laden,
And I will give you rest.
Matthew 11:28

Behold I stand at the door and knock.
If anyone hears My voice and opens the door,
I will come in to him and dine with him,
and he with me.
Revelation 3:20

My sheep hear my voice,
and I know them, and they follow me.
John 10:27

Bandit isn't an obedient dog. He just isn't. He is not particularly rebellious; he just isn't especially obedient, either. He means no harm; he just has a mind of his own. As I mentioned before, he's never learned what "come" means. Actually, he *chooses* to be ignorant of the meaning of "come." You can call, "Bandit, come!" until the cows come home, and all you will get in return is a vacuous stare. He's good at this.

He's an excellent thespian. He *acts* as though he doesn't have a clue, but I *know* he does. He chooses to ignore the command.

Bandit has learned the names of his favorite pooch friends and people friends. For instance, he knows instantly when I say "Monte" and goes running to the front door or window to look for his favorite doggy pal, a Lhasa Apso that Bandit has known almost all his life and has played with often. He does likewise when he hears the name "Sophie," a beautiful mixed breed girlfriend with thick black, curly fur. Bandit has had an eye for her since the first day he met her, shortly after we moved into our home just over two years ago. He recently met a new friend, Rufus, a cute little Papillon. Bandit and Rufus have become best pals and play wildly together. Bandit jumps for joy when I tell him Rufus is coming over to play. He also knows "Uncle Mike" one of his favorite people friends, and of course, "Daddy" (Jim). These names, and a few words (such as toy, blue bear, ball, treat, Buddy Biscuit, pig ear) comprise most of Bandit's vocabulary—as I know it to be. But, apparently, he understands more that I realize.

I noticed something this morning. The more Bandit listens to me—the more he *hears* my voice—the more he *understands*. Conversely, the more he *understands*, the more I can *communicate* with him.

So here's the analogy. I have found that if I quiet myself for only *five minutes*, and just sit at the feet of Jesus, I will hear what He has to say to me. He will give me an insight that is just for me. It happens over and over again. So why don't I just get quiet and listen?

Because, I'm like Bandit. I'm busy with my own stuff. He has toys to play with, sleeping to do, sniffing, running, jumping—all his doggy stuff. He has a multitude of things to occupy his canine time. And, I have a multitude of things to occupy my time, as well. I have phone calls to make, email to check, bills to pay, two home businesses to run, groceries to buy, dinner to fix, dishes to wash, floors to mop, toilets to scrub, windows to wash, television to watch (come on, you know you do, too), and the list goes on and on. I'm exhausted just thinking about it!

I use up precious minutes, hours, days, weeks, months, years (yikes!) just doing stuff—most of which doesn't really matter. If I were not here, if the Lord called me home, all that stuff would get done—if it even needed doing in the first place; *e.g.* no one *really* needs to watch T.V. or read email jokes. This became abundantly clear to me when my mother and stepfather were living out their last days. I was so conscious of how little time they had left. And even though they both suffered from dementia, I think they were aware of how fleeting the time was. They showed no interest in television. Sometimes I would turn it on in their room at the nursing home just to have the sound of it to break the growing silence caused by their illness, and to cover the daily noises of the home. They were not interested in television, and neither was I. It became obvious what a colossal waste of time television really is. So why do I continue to watch it to this day? It's probably more escapism than anything.

But I have found that I can get up in the morning, make some coffee, walk out to the lanai, coffee cup in hand, sit down and have a great conversation with the Lord. It's like sitting in a favorite coffee shop with a wonderful friend. It's not formal ("thee" and "thou") prayer. It's just a conversation with the Creator of the universe. How awesome! (By the way, I'm not a person who uses that word very often. To me, "awesome" should be reserved for things that truly elicit awe—like the attributes of God—not for descriptions of the latest hit song or movie.)

I talk with the Lord, and He talks with me. Isn't that astonishing? Much of the time, I don't say a word. I just get quiet and focus my thoughts on Him, and He starts talking. I am amazed. Why don't I do this more often? Since this wonderful thing happens whenever I just get a cup of coffee and sit down and focus on the Lord, you probably assume that I do this every single morning. Oh, if only that were true. No, I go for weeks, even months, when I don't take the time—when my only communications with God are a quick "thank you" here and there or a frantic yelp for help in the throes of this or that crisis. I'm confessing this because I want you to understand that I'm no spiritual giant. I'm just a person who, from time to time, quiets my mind enough that the Lord can get through with some marvelous insight that He would have me to know. And He shows up! He does it every time. This is such a wonder to me.

Formal prayers leave me cold. I know that the Lord is awesome and that we are to have a certain fear or reverence for Him. But you know what? I "feared" my daddy, yet I loved him and never doubted his love for me. I simply was careful not to sass him or be disrespectful. So when I talk with the Lord, I do so respectfully, but not with fear or dread. Rather, I talk with the Almighty as with my best friend, or with my daddy. My daddy would not have expected me to crawl into his presence or address him with undue formality. After all, I was his *daughter*. I held an exalted position—much lower than his position, but nevertheless much higher than that of a servant or a stranger or even a friend. I was his *daughter*.

I'm reminded of a story I heard about little John-John Kennedy and how he used to run into the Oval Office and climb up into President John Kennedy's lap. I heard that he sometimes did so during important meetings. And his daddy, the President of the mightiest country in the world, suspended what he was doing and took his child into his lap and held him. John-John didn't disrespect his daddy; he didn't even understand how important his daddy was or the office he held. He knew only that this was *his* daddy and that his daddy welcomed him with delight.

For you did not receive the spirit of bondage again to fear, but you received the Spirit of adoption by whom we cry out, "Abba, Father." Romans 8:15. The Aramaic word "Abba," as defined in *Nelson's New Illustrated Bible Dictionary,*[4] is actually a very affectionate, intimate term similar to our word, "daddy." Doesn't it totally blow your mind that the Creator of the Universe calls us His children, and allows us to call Him "Daddy"? Incredible!

I feel the same way about being interrupted by Bandit as, apparently, President Kennedy felt about being interrupted by his beloved son. It's always a joy! This morning, my quiet time with the Lord was indeed intruded upon by Bandit. I noticed that he was staring at me expectantly—wanting to be taken out. Well, some things can't wait, so I left my perch on the lawn chair, and I left my coffee shop with the Lord and took Bandit out in the back yard. When we came back, Bandit went back into the house and plopped down in the family room, grabbing a "chew stick." Chew sticks are bovine tendons that are dried into hard "sticks."

When Bandit realized that I was going to stay outside in the screened lanai, he bounded for the glass door just as I was about to shut it. He was in such a hurry that he abandoned his chew stick. I knew he would want it, so I said to him, "Get your chew stick." I don't know why I told him to do this because, to my knowledge, Bandit didn't know that it was called a "chew stick." I have often referred to it as such when I would give him one, but let's face it, he's a Shih Tzu. While Shih Tzus are loveable and affectionate, no one could ever accuse them of being particularly bright. Bandit is no exception. He is not the smartest dog on the porch.

Nevertheless, when I said "get your chew stick," he went right for it, grabbed it up and ran out into the lanai, jumped into a chair and happily returned to his chewing. I was amazed and I told him so.

"Wow, you knew what I said!"

That's when it occurred to me that Bandit had been *listening* all the other times when I had called it a "chew stick." Then the Lord gave me the insight that I shared at the beginning of this chapter. The more Bandit listens to my voice, the more he understands what I am saying. And the more he understands, the more I can communicate further with him.

In the same way, the more I listen to my Father, abide in His word and ponder His word in my heart, the more I will understand. And as I comprehend more, He can communicate further, so that I discern even more. I don't think this insight would have occurred to me if I hadn't been spending time with my Father. My mind was open to receive. I had been listening.

Oh, Father, that I may be quiet in body and spirit, that I may draw near to You, abide in

*Your presence, and listen to Your voice so that
I may understand and You can tell me more!*

Open my eyes, that I may see
Wondrous things from Your law.
Psalm 119:18

Open my eyes, that I may see,
Glimpses of truth Thou hast for me;
Place in my hands the wonderful key
That shall unclasp and set me free.

Silently now I wait for Thee,
Ready, my God, Thy will to see.
Open my eyes, illumine me,
Spirit divine.
From Open My Eyes, That I May See
A hymn by Clara H. Scott, 1895

Chapter Nine
Persistence!

... yet because of his persistence he will rise and give
him [what] he needs
Luke 11:8b

I am lying in bed one afternoon reading a book and
hoping to drop off to sleep for a short power nap—having
awakened at four that morning in a panic and unable to go back
to sleep. I was panicking over the housing market in the United
States, in general, and in Florida in particular, *i.e.*, I had
"buyer's remorse" over the recent purchase of the two
investment houses mentioned in Chapter Five. The previous
day we had gotten a "doom and gloom" flyer in the mail
predicting that the "housing bubble" was about to burst, and on
the evening news, there was speculation that interest rates were
about to go up and concern over what rising interest would do
to the, presumed fragile, housing market boom. That news was
fresh on my mind as I went to sleep a little after midnight. It's

no wonder that I awoke in a blind panic at 4:00 a.m.

So I had gotten up and started my day at that ghastly hour. By two o'clock in the afternoon, I was bushed and ready for a nap. But at my age naps don't come easily. In fact, sleep at any time in any form doesn't come easily. I have found that I can manage quite well on about six hours of sleep—but four hours just doesn't cut it. I had finally taken to my bed with a good book in the hopes that a little nap would sneak up on me. That's when I heard it—Bandit on the floor on the other side of the bed alternately whimpering ever so slightly and then growling a little low growl. I tried to block him out, but he kept on.

Finally, I threw back the covers, crawled to the other side of the bed and peered over the edge. There was Bandit, lying on the floor staring intently at something and growling. I noticed Jim's little black flashlight on the floor and mistakenly thought that it was the subject of Bandit's complaint. If anything unusual comes into Bandit's kingdom, he investigates it gingerly, and if he still doesn't understand it, he will growl at it in an effort to rid his domain of the offending object. I discovered this propensity in Bandit one morning when we were out for a walk. Overnight, it seems, a large white mushroom had sprung up in a neighbor's yard across the street. Bandit stopped dead in his tracks in our driveway and growled at the impertinent mushroom. How dare it be in his territory!

When I saw the flashlight on the floor, I assumed it was a "mushroom"—so I picked it up and put it on Jim's night stand.

The growling continued—punctuated every now and then by a little whimper or two. Again, I tried to ignore it, telling Bandit, "It's just a flashlight. Get over it!"He would have none of it. He continued his growling/whining resolve.

Trust me, it's very difficult to fall asleep with little doggy noises in your immediate vicinity. Actually, it's impossible. So I threw back the covers *again*, dragged myself to the other side of the bed *again*, and peered over the edge *again*. This time, I realized that whatever it was that had Bandit's complete attention was not on the floor *by* the bed; it actually was *under* it. So I climbed down off the bed and peeked under it. Ours is a converted water bed for which Jim had built a wooden frame about thirty-five years ago. When we decided to get rid of the water bed bladder and go back to a regular mattress, Jim put plywood across the top of the wooden frame, with braces every few feet so that it wouldn't sag, and we plopped the mattress on top of it. It makes for a *really firm* bed, but we like it. There are wooden supports that run across the head and foot underneath the bed. As I stared into the darkness, I noticed one of Bandit's toys almost hidden behind one of the supports. There's only a small space between the support, the night stand and the wall—a space too small for Bandit to crawl through. He could see his toy, but he couldn't reach it. So, of course, I retrieved it for him and he gleefully grabbed it and started his favorite activity, as with any toy—shaking the dickens out of it! Maybe he was trying to teach it a lesson for getting itself stuck under the bed.

Problem solved, I settled back down with my book. Bandit climbed up next to me and settled himself down, happily hanging on tightly to his prize. I figured he would follow his usual routine—play with the toy for a while, and then fall asleep on top of it. After a short time, however, he started to make little noises *again*. This time, he wasn't growling or even whining—just making barely perceptible little noises. Can you imagine how annoying that is when you are trying to drop off to sleep? Just as your eyes get heavy, there's a tiny little noise. You almost wonder if you actually heard something or not. You close your eyes again, and then there it is again—just a teensy, weensy noise.

Finally, I look at Bandit. He looks back with that "I've got a problem" look on his face. Now, there are people who will tell you that a dog's face cannot show expression. *Au contraire.* I can look at Bandit and see in his face when something is wrong—or when he's excited, has to go out, wants a treat, doesn't feel well—you name it, I can see it in his face. It's because I know him very well, and his looks—though subtle—are distinct.

I realize, *again*, that he is staring at (or at least toward) something. This time, he is staring toward the head of the bed. Because this is a converted waterbed, there is a good-sized gap between the mattress and the headboard. I've lost many a pillow over that edge during the night. Then I notice that Bandit no longer has his toy, and I figure it out. Sure enough, it has gone through the gap and ended up under the bed again. It's probably how it got there the first time. I remember that Bandit had the toy in bed a couple of nights ago. He had probably lost it over the edge then, and now he has done it again. So, of course, I reach down to the floor between the headboard and the wood frame and retrieve his beloved toy.

It's at this point that I suddenly remember the parable Jesus told right after He taught his disciples how to pray—giving them the model prayer, known as "The Lord's Prayer" in Luke 11:2-4. Right after that, in Luke 11:5-8, Jesus tells the parable of the friend who comes at midnight asking his neighbor for bread to be able to serve an unexpected late-night visitor who has come to him after a long journey. If you've ever made bread—even with that modern wonder called a bread maker—you know that it's no short project. Bread, if you are out of it, is not something you can hustle up at midnight to serve an unanticipated guest. Since there was no local Publix or Albertson's or Kroger, the needy man had nowhere to turn but to his sleeping neighbor.

The scripture says that the neighbor heard the knocking

on his front door and responded "from within" saying, "Do not trouble me; the door is now shut, and my children are with me in bed; I cannot rise and give to you." (I can't help but notice that even in Bible times, children—and perhaps pets—allowed into the parents' bed seemed to remain there, just as Bandit remains in ours!)

So what happens? The guy keeps knocking; that's what happens! This man is desperate. He has a guest; and in that culture (maybe in *any* culture) it was considered extremely rude not to serve something to a visitor—albeit an unexpected one—and especially one worn out from a long journey. So he continues to knock and plead with his neighbor. And guess what? The neighbor gets out of bed, goes to the kitchen, gets the bread for his friend and gives it to him. The scripture tells us that the reward is for his *persistence*. Luke 11:8: . . . *though he will not rise and give to him because he is his friend, yet because of his persistence he will rise and give him as many [loaves of bread] as he needs.*

Frankly, I've often wondered about the persistence described in that parable and in a parable with a similar theme (regarding the widow and the "unjust judge") in Luke 18:2-7. The Lord prefaces that parable by saying in Luke 18:1 that we should "*always* pray and not lose heart." I have wondered why it is necessary for us to continue to ask when Matthew 6:8 tells us that our Father knows our needs before we even ask. So if

God loves us (and we know that He does) and if He already knows our needs before we ask (and we are assured that He does), why do we need to persist? Why, indeed?

Well, I love Bandit. If there's such a thing as loving too much, I come pretty dang close to it with Bandit. I love that little guy with every fiber in my being. And I often know his needs before he asks (begs, whimpers, growls). As I described before, I understand "the look." He can look at me, and I just know what it is that he needs. So why does he have to persist in asking? Well, maybe it's because I lead a busy life and I'm absorbed with lots of stuff that really doesn't involve Bandit, or maybe as in the case in point, I'm trying to rest or attend to some other need of my own, or Jim's, or a friend's, or a son's, or a grandchild's or a multitude of others—all vying for my attention. It's not that I don't care about Bandit's needs, but it just may be that there are other pressing matters ahead of his needs at the moment.

Perhaps we don't like to think that God is not at our beck and call. But, after all, He *is* the Creator of the heavens (everything out there!) and earth. And He keeps it all running in perfect precision. So He just might have a few other things to do when we start our growling and whimpering. Romans 8:34 assures us that the Son sits at the right hand of the Father to make intercession for us. But, hey, there are LOTS of us! Maybe we need to persist so that our particular concern gets its proper place in the queue.

I'm sure He can "read" our moods and desires infinitesimally better than I can read Bandit's. So He easily discerns the difference between the urgent, desperate "I need help *NOW!*" cry and the "Hey, there's something that's troubling me" cry. We rest in the knowledge that we can skid to our knees in a flash and urgently cry out to our Father and He can, and does, answer in a nanosecond. We are not talking about those kinds of emergencies here. We are talking about those day-in, day-out nagging needs that trouble us. The "my-toy-is-under-the-bed-and-I-can't-reach-it" whimpers.

Maybe I'm way off base here theologically, but it helps me understand why I need to continue to bring my petitions to the Lord and to persist. To me, the admonition in Luke 18:1 that "Men ought always to pray and not lose heart" is the scriptural version of "the squeaky wheel gets the oil." Bandit demonstrated it to me, and now I get it.

Chapter Ten
Good Old Fashioned Foot Washing

After that he poureth water into a basin,
and began to wash the disciples' feet, and to wipe them
with the towel wherewith he was girded.
Then cometh he to Simon Peter:
- - - - -
Peter saith unto him, Thou shalt never wash my feet.
Jesus answered him,
If I wash thee not, thou hast no part with me.
Simon Peter saith unto him,
Lord, not my feet only, but also my hands and my head.
John 13:5-6a; 8-9 (KJV)

Peter answered and said unto him,
Though all men shall be offended because of thee,
yet will I never be offended.
Jesus said unto him, Verily I say unto thee,
That this night, before the cock crow,
thou shalt deny me thrice.
Peter said unto him, Though I should die with thee,
yet will I not deny thee.
Matthew 26:33-35a (KJV)

Then began he to curse and to swear, saying,
I know not the man.

And immediately the cock crew.
And Peter remembered the word of Jesus,
which said unto him,
Before the cock crow, thou shalt deny me thrice.
And he went out, and wept bitterly.
Matthew 26: 74-75 (KJV)

And Peter answered him and said,
Lord, if it be thou, bid me come unto thee on the water.
And he said, Come.
And when Peter was come down out of the ship,
he walked on the water, to go to Jesus.
But when he saw the wind boisterous, he was afraid;
and beginning to sink, he cried, saying, Lord, save me.
And immediately Jesus stretched forth his hand,
and caught him, and said unto him,
O thou of little faith, wherefore didst thou doubt?
Matthew 14:28-31 (KJV)

Then Simon Peter having a sword drew it,
and smote the high priest's servant, and cut off his right ear.
The servant's name was Malchus.
Then said Jesus unto Peter,
Put up thy sword into the sheath:
the cup which my Father hath given me,
shall I not drink it?
John 18:10-11 (KJV)

We live in Florida, land of the perpetually *wet* grass. Every morning when I take Bandit out for his first walk, the grass is heavily laden with the previous night's dew. And, of course, we get thunderstorms almost daily in the summer and much rain in the winter as well. So, very often when I take Bandit out, his feet get wet, muddy and grimy. Sometimes there are little pieces of cut grass matted in his fur from his walking through freshly mown (and *wet*) yards. Often, then, the ritual on our return home is a good foot washing!

I was doing the routine foot washing the other morning and talking to Bandit about it as I tackled the task. I always put him in the utility sink in the laundry room. Eons ago, when I was in grade school, a good friend of mine taught me a horrific, little ditty about "great green gobs of greasy, grimy gopher guts, mutilated monkey meat, dirty little birdie feet." Just the sort of song that every mother wants her eight or nine-year-old budding young lady to learn! Anyway, while I am washing Bandit's feet, I often sing to him about (as I revise it) "dirty little *puppy* feet." I don't include the rest of the refrain. I wish I could erase the memory tape of it! That morning as I was washing his feet and singing to him about "dirty little puppy feet,"my mind went to a phrase I had often heard while growing up in the South, "a good old-fashioned foot-washing!"

Many of the churches in the old South would have good old-fashioned foot-washings from time to time. I have been witness to several foot washings—not only in the old South—but also in other places and settings. In all instances, they have been very meaningful experiences. One that was particularly meaningful happened only a few years ago while I was at a weekend Christian retreat. A husband, in great honor of his wife, brought a basin to where she was seated. Then he knelt before her, towel draped around his neck, and lovingly washed and dried her feet. My eyes are filled with tears as I write this. That's how meaningful and fresh this event has remained in my memory.

As I continued to think about foot-washings that morning while I washed dirty little puppy feet, I thought of Jesus and the Twelve and how He humbled himself and girded His precious body with a towel, knelt down and washed their feet. I'm told that in those days it was common for Jewish households in the often dusty land of Israel to have arriving guests' feet washed by a servant. It is mind-boggling to think that the God of all creation humbled Himself as a servant, and washed His friends' feet. As I continued my reverie, I thought of Peter—good old, impetuous Peter. I thought of how he at first refused to have his feet washed by the Lord. But when Jesus said that if He did not wash his feet, he would have no part with Him, Peter responded, "Lord, not my feet only, but also my hands and my head."

I find it so encouraging that Peter was one of the chosen apostles, and I'm so glad that his story—with all its shortcomings—is included in the New Testament. Being an impulsive person myself, I can identify so much with Peter. He was always brashly stepping up to the plate only to be gently reminded of his own frailty and the Lord's authority.

I think of Peter jumping out of the boat to walk on the

water when he saw Jesus coming toward the apostles' little ship—walking on rough seas. And of Peter sinking when he took his eyes off the Lord and looked in fear at the raging waters instead.

I think of Peter, on the night Jesus was betrayed, brandishing a sword and cutting off the ear of the high priest's servant and Jesus gently restoring the ear.

It invariably brings tears to my eyes whenever I read of Peter's denial (for the third time that evening) of even knowing the Lord and immediately hearing the rooster crow. How devastated Peter must have been as he remembered that Jesus had predicted he would deny Him three times that very night before the rooster crowed.

I love these stories about Peter because they remind me that even when I fall down by defaulting on promises, or failing to trust, or not doing enough, or doing too much, or loving too little or too much—no matter how I fail, the Lord is there to patiently remedy the trouble I have caused and gently restore me to fellowship with Him. What a gracious, loving God we serve!

All of these thoughts were swirling through my mind just as the water swirled down the drain taking away the dirt and grime and grass clippings from Bandit's feet. It occurred to me that I was washing Bandit's feet because I love him intensely. I love him so much that I don't want him to have itchy, grass fungus between his toes. I don't want him to have fleas that might have jumped onto his feet and legs as he waded through the grass sniffing, ever sniffing here and there. I use a special soap on his feet—one that is non-toxic and yet it kills germs and fungus and even fleas. I do all this because I desperately love this little dog, and I want him to have the best life possible.

Isn't that what the Lord wants for me? Isn't that what He wants for you? Isn't that why He gave us the loving example of humbling Himself and washing the disciples' feet—even Peter's feet? No matter how much I love a little dog, it cannot even begin to compare to the vast love that God has for me. Yet, my love for Bandit gives me a tiny, infinitesimal glimpse of what God's love for me must be like. And I caught this glimpse while washing dirty little puppy feet.

Chapter Eleven
I Am Loved, After All

And now abide faith, hope, love, these three;
but the greatest of these is love.
1 Cor. 13:13

I'm intrigued when I hear someone talk of how they came from a "dysfunctional" home. To some extent, didn't we all? I have to wonder whether there are, in fact, any *functional* homes. Doesn't everyone have memories of homes that were less than ideal, childhoods that were far from perfect? Yet many of us labor under the misapprehension that we had wonderful childhoods until some life event suddenly pulls back the curtain and we see our past more clearly. Such was my experience when my mother and stepfather passed away. I found myself contemplating the past and examining what I found there.

Grief has a way of causing one to reflect on the past. While unhappy memories may lurk in the subconscious, emotionally stable people usually do not dwell on them. The memories are there, but they don't play a major role in our everyday lives. That is, until someone dies. Then the floodgates open, and memories—good ones, bad ones, happy ones, unhappy ones—spill to the forefront of the minds and emotions of the surviving relatives and friends. It has been postulated, by persons much wiser than I, that a significant part of grief is *regret*. It is painful examination of the past and remorse over lost opportunities to express love for and appreciation of the one who has departed.

Many of us came from admittedly dysfunctional homes or from homes that seemed functional until examined under the intense illumination of grief. This chapter is for those who have been, or are presently, a part of such a home. My prayer is that you will gain insight into the powerful emotional currents that make up every family, that you will forgive those who may have churned those currents in your own family, and that you will forgive yourself for any failure, or perceived failure, on your own part. I pray for the sweet release that only such forgiveness can bring.

Until I ended up in counseling, I had always thought that I had somewhat of an idyllic childhood. As I explored my past in therapy, however, I came to realize that I may not have had flawless parents or a perfect home life. I was exceedingly blessed to have been born in a free country to parents who were Christian and who taught me about the Lord and took me to church to learn more about Him. What more could I ask? Well, how about *love*? Love that is *spoken* and *demonstrated*.

Years ago, I happened to read about a 1958 experiment done with baby monkeys. Dr. Harry F. Harlow of the University of Wisconsin did numerous studies with baby rhesus monkeys. In one study, Dr. Harlow put a replica of a mother monkey at one end of a cage. The replica was made of wood and covered with soft foam and terry cloth. A light was installed inside the "monkey" so that it felt warm. At the other end of the cage, Dr. Harlow put a wire mesh "monkey." Although this replica was also fitted with a warm light, its structure was hard to the touch. Two small groups of baby monkeys were used in the experiment. One group was taught to receive their nourishment from a milk-dispensing apparatus attached to the soft "monkey." The other group was taught to receive nourishment from the same type apparatus attached to the wire mesh "monkey." Dr. Harlow discovered that, unless the babies were hungry, *both* groups of baby monkeys stayed huddled against the soft monkey replica. Only when driven by hunger would the second group go to the wire-mesh monkey at the other end of the cage. Once their hunger was satisfied, they would return to the soft one.

Here is what I learned from that story: My mother was wire-mesh. Although she took excellent care of my needs, I never felt any softness about her during my childhood and youth. It was not until late in my adult life that I really began to feel love and warmth from my mother. She softened, and I softened in response. I am so grateful that God allowed me to see this side of her before she passed away.

My mother was domineering, and my father was passive. Daddy worked, and he worked hard. Mother also worked and worked hard. They were both in retail—Daddy was a butcher and Mother sold shoes in a local store owned by the Krugers, a Jewish family. Most of the stores in our little town of Fitzgerald, Georgia were owned by Jews. Most of the members of the local country club were Jewish. Our little town even had a synagogue—pretty unusual in those days for a small community in the Deep South. I remember that the rabbi's name was Nathan Cohen. He used to have a radio program, and I often listened to it. I grew up having no concept whatsoever of antisemitism. I was well into my adulthood before I ever even heard the word. I grew up knowing nothing about Jews except to love and respect them. The Krugers treated us like their own family.

Some of my fondest memories were times I spent at the shoe store while Mother worked. Reuben and Connie never seemed to mind my hanging around the store. After I grew up, moved away and had children of my own, we would often descend on the store when we arrived in town for a weekend visit. Reuben and Connie would greet us as if I were their own daughter bringing the grandchildren for a visit.

Daddy was a meat market manager of a grocery store that was part of a small chain in the southeast. He arose every weekday morning before dawn and was at work just as the sun was coming up. He got home well after dark each night. Daddy was extremely thin and as such, he was exceptionally sensitive to cold weather. It seemed a cruel trick of fate that most of his life was spent working inside a refrigerated market where cold meat hung on enormous hooks. When he wasn't in the refrigerated area, he was in the freezer locker retrieving frozen slabs of meat. So his days were spent going from "cold" to "colder."

He loved the bright days of summer, and hated winter. His heart's desire was to move to Florida and bask in warm sunshine. And, thank God, he achieved his dream in 1970, when he was fifty-eight years old. He and Mother moved to Charlotte County, and he got a job at a local supermarket. He was shocked when upper management there insisted that he take two fifteen-minute breaks a day! Daddy hardly knew what to do with all that extra personal time. He had never in his entire life had a break at work. He started taking little snacks to work with him, as a way to fill the time on the breaks. Mother got a job selling shoes in a department store, and she later became the manager of the shoe department there.

While we were living in Fitzgerald, Daddy and Mother

had worked five and a half days a week. They had Sundays off and Wednesday afternoons—when the entire town shut down. Any clement Wednesday afternoon would find my parents working in the yard. I can remember them practically diving into old clothes as soon as they came in the door, so that they could hurry out into the yard and get to work—digging around in the flower beds, weeding and working the ground. They managed without the most remedial lawn implements. Daddy mowed the yard with an unpowered push mower, and he did not have an edger. Instead he worked his way around the perimeter of the yard and all the flower beds on his hands and knees with a meat cleaver hacking away at the stubborn grass that persistently threatened to invade all the gardens. He didn't even have a decent meat cleaver. The one he used in the yard was one that was no longer of any use in the store—because it had no protective wood on the metal handle. Daddy tied a rag around it so that the metal wouldn't dig into his hand.

Besides yard work, there were all kinds of other chores for a Wednesday afternoon. Daddy often went to the sawmill to get a load of sawdust for the floor of the meat market. He did this on his only afternoon off and would pile the sawdust into the trunk of his own car. I went with him. I loved the pungent scent of the freshly sawn wood at the sawmill.

When the yard work was done, Mother would cook and clean indoors. Sometimes she would bake something scrumptious. She baked without even rudimentary baking utensils. She had no measuring cups and no measuring spoons. She eye-balled everything—roughly estimating how much a cup of this, or a ½ teaspoon of that, would be. Despite the paucity of utensils, her baking was consistently delicious.

On Saturday nights, the stores were open late. (I think until nine.) Closing time on Monday, Tuesday, Thursday and Friday was six in the evening and on Wednesday at noon. On Saturday nights, Daddy sometimes got a call to make a delivery to the Spotted Pig restaurant on the other side of town. Daddy could never refuse a request from as good and steady a customer as the Spotted Pig. So he would personally deliver whatever the restaurant needed to get through the weekend. While he was there, he would pick up some supper—to go. He would bring home a gastronomic delight—hamburgers and chocolate milk! I would put a pin hole in the aluminum foil cap on the glass chocolate milk bottle and suck the contents out ever so slowly—to make it last as long as possible. I didn't want the special treat to end.

This was "love" in the only way I understood at that time. "Love" was demonstrated when someone brought me something. And that someone was usually Daddy. He brought me ginger ale whenever I was sick. He brought me hamburgers and chocolate milk from the Saturday night run to the Spotted Pig. He took me to the dime store to buy doll clothes for my doll. Daddy was seldom ever away from home, but on the rare occasion when he was required to go out of town, he always brought something back for me.

To this day, my only real concept of love is all wrapped up in the act of giving. The imprint I got from my childhood is that love involves giving. Even as an adult, I still harbor the suspicion that someone who never gives me anything, could not possibly love me. I think it's one reason that it was so easy for me to believe and accept God's supreme gift. The gift of His only Son for me—and for you and for everyone who will accept the marvelous free gift. *Thanks be to God for His unspeakable gift*, 2 Corinthians 9:15 (KJV).

Daddy also gave me something much more valuable than chocolate milk, hamburgers, ginger ale, doll clothes and other tokens. He gave me his time. The happiest times I remember from my childhood were those I spent with Daddy. He took me to football games and baseball games. I knew almost nothing about either sport, but I loved going with Daddy and eating hotdogs and peanuts.

Daddy took me swimming at Bowen's Mill—a public swimming pool located about ten miles from town at the site of an old grist mill. Originally, the decaying old paddle wheel and mill house were there, but eventually the decay won the battle. There was a sharp curve in the road and a decline just before the entrance to Bowen's Mill. I daresay that everyone who grew up in Fitzgerald remembers the phrase, "Around the curve and down the hill, and here we are at Bowen's Mill."

Daddy took my sister and my cousin Rudolph and me on a trip to the mountains in the Carolinas and Virginia, and to the beach there. I was about six years old at the time. We went to Norfolk, Virginia, to visit my grandmother who was living there at the time with Daddy's brother. My most frightening remembrance of the trip was my getting lost on Virginia Beach. I can still see in my mind the relief on Daddy's and Granny's faces when they finally discovered me walking along the beach, crying at the top of my lungs.

Looking back, I realize that we could ill afford to travel. We stayed in small roadside "motor courts" and stopped at picnic tables along the way to eat such sumptuous fare as Vienna sausage, potted meat and crackers. We loudly and repeatedly sang "In the Blue Ridge Mountains of Virginia and the Trail of the Lonesome Pine." It was the only line that any of us knew from the song, and we sang it continually until everyone in the car was thoroughly fed up with hearing it. We stopped at numerous craft shops featuring lawn ornaments—Daddy's weakness. He seldom ever spent money, but lawn ornaments were an indulgence he could not deny himself. We brought back a large, heavy green frog made of concrete and a little decorative wooden wheelbarrow to adorn our yard. We also got two "flying geese"—large wooden birds mounted on top of poles with wings that turned like windmills. We were all fascinated with the countless rock slides, so in addition to the yard treasures, we brought back with us what seemed like tons of rocks. I'm sure our gas mileage on the return trip was much worse than on the outbound one.

When I was in high school, Daddy took me and two of my friends to Atlanta and on up into north Georgia (to the mountains again) for a short trip. We visited the state Capitol in Atlanta and the Cyclorama—a huge circular painting melding into a three-dimensional diorama complete with wax figures depicting the July 22, 1864, Battle of Atlanta.

Daddy not only gave his time to Sylvia and me, but to other kids as well. From my earliest remembrances, Daddy taught Sunday School. He also led a troop of Royal Ambassadors (the R.A.'s), a boys' Christian organization in our church. He formed a "Sword Team"—a group of adolescents who competed with other Sword Teams around the state in proficiency drills on swiftness in finding scripture. I remember many an evening when the Sword Team practiced in our living room, getting ready for the next competition.

Daddy was always giving—of his time, of his money, of himself. He was the soft, fuzzy one.

In sharp contrast to Daddy, Mother treated me with business-like efficiency. I didn't interpret this as love. But I didn't interpret it as lack of love, either. I made absolutely no emotional connection to it. And I felt lonely all the time. Mother made clothes for my sister and me. She often made matching Easter outfits for us. If Easter came early and the weather was predicted to be cool, she would make dusters to match our outfits. She saw to it that we both got piano and voice lessons—although in retrospect, I realize now that we could barely afford such a luxury. I remember many a gentle reminder from Mrs. Wimpee that payment was due for the lessons.

Mother saw to it that we made regular visits to the dentist. I can thank her that I have good teeth to this day. She cooked and cleaned and made sure we were well fed and had clean clothes to wear. I never interpreted any of this as love. I never actually "felt" anything warm and soft from her—just functional.

My sister, seven years older than me, tended to my care—dressing me, bathing me, teaching me, reading and singing to me. I don't recall my mother ever actually touching me when I was a child, except to give me a spanking or a smack on the bottom if I misbehaved. The only other "touch" I recall was on Sunday mornings in the car on the way to church. We went to church *every* Sunday. Daddy was a deacon, the Sunday school superintendent, and a "pillar" at the local First Baptist Church. We always arrived early because Daddy had self-imposed duties. Mother used to quip that Daddy had to get there early to "dust out the pews." And we always stayed late. Again, because of Daddy's duties. He stood at the back door shaking hands with the departing congregation while the preacher was at the front door doing the same.

As we rode along in the old Plymouth on the way to church, Mother would turn around and inspect my eyes, for "sleepers" in the corners, and the rest of my face for any remaining traces of breakfast. If any offending sleepers or dried egg or toast crumbs were discovered, she would dab a Kleenex on her tongue and wipe various areas around my eyes and/or mouth. I always hated this Sunday morning ritual. (And, by the way, we used "Kleenex," not "tissues." I never heard the term "tissue" until I became an adult.)

The idea of anyone in my family ever actually "loving" another family member was too uncomfortable a subject ever to be broached. I vividly recall one Mother's Day when the preacher announced that children all over the congregation should go stand by their mothers for a special prayer. The mere announcement filled me with apprehension. I was probably around thirteen or fourteen years old at the time. I was in the choir, so I descended from the choir loft, dutifully found my mother and stood stiffly beside her—dreading whatever was to come. The preacher asked that all the children hold hands with their mothers as he prayed the special prayer for us. I was mortified! I could not imagine holding my mother's hand under any circumstances whatsoever. My face flushed crimson as I felt her hand take mine. The preacher prayed, and I prayed for his prayer to end quickly so that I could get my hand back. As soon as I heard "amen," I dropped my mother's hand like a hot poker! I had never held her hand before, and she had never held mine. We simply were not a demonstrative family.

"Love" was a foreign, never-used term in our house. Perhaps it was the times. The idea of love was not bandied about the way it is today. People were more reserved and formal. Not as open in expressing affection. At least, that's the way it was in our home. Daddy would kiss my forehead or my cheek when I went to bed at night. I actually dreaded the kiss. The dampness left on my head or cheek was disconcerting. As soon as Daddy left the room, I would wipe off the objectionable moisture. I don't recall my mother ever kissing me at all. I'm sure I would have found it equally distasteful.

I have often said that my Daddy "poured himself out like a drink offering" for his family.

> *Yes, and if I am being poured out as a drink offering on the sacrifice and service of your faith, I am glad and rejoice with you all.*
> Philippians 2:17

Although Daddy worked constantly, I never knew him to have more than a dollar in his pocket. He brought his paycheck home to the family, and as far as he was concerned, that was the end of it. We had needs, and he did what he could to meet them. Because he was so giving, I always thought of Daddy as a loving man. He addressed Mother and Sylvia and me with loving pet names—"sugar" was his favorite term of endearment. When he called "sugar," none of the three of us knew whom he meant, so we all responded. Yet I never heard the words "I love you" come from his lips.

My mother was finally able to say "I love you" to me in her later years. Perhaps she learned something about demonstrative love from my stepfather. Perhaps it was just the fact that I continued to tell her that I loved her. I don't know. But she finally did arrive at a point where she could say the words.

In contrast to my biological parents, my stepfather was openly affectionate. I fell in love with him the first day I met him. My mother had "summoned" me to her home in Port Charlotte to meet her new beau, Herbert Borleis. Prior to that day, I had spoken once with Herb on the phone when I happened to call Mother one evening and she nervously explained that she had a boyfriend and that he was there at her home at the time. She abruptly placed him on the phone, and we made the kind of strained small talk that complete strangers make when thrust into such an awkward situation. He had a soft, pleasant voice; I can still hear it today in my mind.

The moment I actually met in person with the man who

was to become my new dad, I felt immediately at ease. He had a disarmingly warm smile and a kind face. He was relatively portly, and a little shorter than my mother. My daddy, on the other hand, had been inordinately thin and just about Mother's height. Standing at five feet six inches, my mother was rather tall for a woman of her generation. She was a beautiful woman. Her great-grandmother had been a Cherokee Indian, and Mother had the characteristic high cheekbones, brown eyes and black hair. In her youth, she had the kind of beauty that elicits attention. Heads turned when she walked into a room. Even at age sixty-eight (at the time) she was still beautiful. The years had only softened her lovely features. Her dark eyes shown, and her face was fringed with curly, silver-gray hair. Her high cheekbones still gave her an exotic beauty that time had dealt with kindly.

Mother and her new suitor made a handsome pair. I remember thinking how youthful Herb looked for his eighty years. He was pleasantly handsome and could easily have been mistaken for mid-sixty. He had no problem at all in showing and expressing affection. Perhaps his complete comfort with closeness was the result of his traumatic childhood. His mother had died in the influenza pandemic of 1918. Herb was only twelve years old when his mother died. He was shuttled off to live with an aunt and uncle, where he felt that he was an unwanted burden. Perhaps it was the sheer loneliness of that experience that created such a warmth and depth of spirit in him. Whatever it was, my new dad was a sweet, kind, affectionate father to me.

I never knew Dad to be in a bad mood. Whenever I saw him, he was always "up." He greeted me with a warm smile, a hug and a kiss. After he and Mother had passed away, I often went back in memory to the times when I would arrive at their front door and be greeted so lovingly. I envisioned all the furniture, the layout of the living room, the piano, the organ, the pictures on the walls, the chiming clock, Mother and Dad smiling, delighted to see me. And, in my mind's eye, I also could see clearly all the goodbyes, with Dad standing in the front yard waving and saying, "C.B.S. Come back soon." I imagine being greeted so sweetly when I join them again in heaven. But, this time, there will be no goodbyes.

I recall the night when I got a call from the nursing home saying that Dad was in the hospital having suffered a heart attack. This was about a week before he died. I raced to the hospital and found him on a gurney in the emergency room. It was cold in the E.R., and he was covered with only a light blanket. As he would move, the blanket would slip down a bit, exposing his bare shoulders. Each time, I would pull it back up and snug it around his neck, and each time, he would say, "Thank you," and smile at me. He spoke with such gratitude in his voice that it brings tears even now as I think about it.

I have heard that Alzheimer's patients can develop a mean personality and can be extremely difficult to handle. That never happened with Dad. It seems as though the worse his mind became, the sweeter his spirit. Even when gravely ill in the hospital, he was careful to notice and thank me for such a small gesture as adjusting his blanket. Herb was my dad for almost fourteen years. I am so grateful to him, and I miss him terribly

In happier times, we had enjoyed a wonderful celebration when Dad's ninetieth birthday rolled around. Our families joined together and threw him a huge birthday bash. It was a beautiful time of sweet fellowship. Many family members and friends wrote Dad letters describing what he meant to us. Here is my letter verbatim:

Dear Dad,

I have been calling you "Dad" for almost nine years now, and you have filled the part admirably. I am proud to call you Dad, and I am so happy that you came into my mother's life, and into my life.

I had a wonderful father. He was my "Daddy," and I was a daddy's girl. I loved him dearly, and I have no doubt that he loved me just as dearly. No one could or can ever replace him. When you took over the job as "Dad" to me, you took on a tall order. But you rose to the challenge. You haven't replaced my Daddy—no one ever can, but you have made the pain of losing him much easier to bear.

Even if you had not done so—even if I didn't even like you, I would still be forever grateful for the light you brought to my mother's eyes at a time when I thought she might not ever smile with her heart again. She really went into a tailspin after Daddy passed away, and I worried that she might just fade away from us, herself. You came along and filled up her life again. You gave her a reason to smile and to laugh and sing and be happy again. Thank you, dear man.

So I decided to call you "Dad." Not "Daddy," because no matter how much I love you, no matter how wonderful I think you are, you are not my daddy. My daddy is with Jesus, the only one he loved more than me and Sylvia and Mama. But you, dear, gentle, sweet man, are the closest second we could ever have found to fill in for our daddy.

Thank you for becoming a part of our family. Thank you for loving us and accepting our love in return. Thank you for loving our mother.

God bless you as we celebrate this 90th

birthday with you. We rejoice that God has allowed you to spend these golden years with us. We pray that he grants you many more good, joy-filled years.

I love you, Dad.
Fran.

Dad and I had bonded almost immediately. Maybe it's because we shared a kinship of having felt unwanted as a child. Maybe those old scars, though deep under the surface of our adult psyches, caused us to gravitate to each other.

Dad had lived with relatives after his mother's untimely death, and he had felt the loneliness of being an extra burden to his aunt and uncle. I, on the other hand, had been unwanted by my own mother from the very beginning. I had been an unexpected, undesired pregnancy. Mother never made any attempt to hide that fact from me. I heard her many times recount how she had angrily thrown her diaphragm in the trash when she realized she was pregnant!

I often heard Mother relate that being pregnant with me had made her so angry that she decided to eat until she became huge. She said that she made a bread pudding every day and ate the whole thing. (I love bread pudding to this day!) Before I was born, she weighed over two hundred pounds. Upon leaving the doctor's office one day late in her pregnancy, she went by the store where Daddy worked and told him her weight. In those days, they had immense scales in the market used for weighing sides of beef. Daddy put Mother on the meat scales and weighed her himself—just to make sure. I was a whopping ten pounds when I was born, so I was probably a difficult birth which, no doubt, only amplified my mother's displeasure at having another child.

I remember laughing as Mother told the story of the trashed diaphragm and her extraordinary weight gain. I don't remember feeling hurt over being unwanted. How is that possible? I think I just willed myself to be impervious to it. As I grew older and began to look back and remember, then I started to hurt. But I forgave my mother, and (I thought) moved on. It was not until I was in counseling and prompted to look back—not as an adult who understands what my mother's life was like, but as a child—that I began to recognize how wounded I was. I was urged to get in touch with what my heart had felt as a toddler and young girl. That's when my heart broke.

My mother and I became good friends as she entered her sixties and we remained so until her death. We often went places together and had the ease of laughter and spontaneity that is so effortless between close friends. It was a sweet time that the Lord blessed us with before Mother went home to Him. I remember a morning when Jim and I sat across from Mother and Dad in a little restaurant we used to frequent together called

Georgio's. We were working from home, so our schedules were flexible enough to allow us the time to make the drive to Port Charlotte for breakfast. We did this about once a week during the last few years of my parents' life. This particular morning, I reached across the table and took one of their hands in each of mine. I smiled into their faces and said, "I want you to know that I feel so honored to be able to spend this time with you. These times are so precious to me, and I just want you to know how much I love being able to get together with you like this."

So there I was, holding my Mother's hand, and my Dad's—and loving it—in sharp contrast to that Mother's Day long ago when I stood stiffly by my mother in church and recoiled at the idea of taking her hand. God had worked a miracle in my heart and in hers. We had become close in those last years of her life, and I thank God for it.

Something occurred to me a few weeks ago. I remembered that when I went to look at the cute Shih Tzu puppies, I did not want a dog. I had no intention of getting a dog. Yet, I did get a dog, and I love him inordinately. That's when God gently suggested to me that my mother actually loved me the same way. When she got me, she really had no intention of having another baby, and did not want a baby. Yet, she came to love me. When I consider how much I love Bandit now, and yet I didn't want a dog that day when I first went to look at puppies, I realize that love is truly a wonderful gift from

God. It can grow even in a heart set against it. It can sneak up on us when we least expect it—and we can love without setting out to do so.

Chapter Twelve
The Power of Words

A continual dripping on a very rainy day
And a contentious woman are alike;
Whoever restrains her restrains the wind,
And grasps oil with his right hand.
Proverbs 27:15-16

It is better to dwell in a corner of a housetop,
Than in a house shared with a contentious woman.
Proverbs 25:24

Whoever guards his mouth and tongue
Keeps his soul from troubles.
Proverbs 21:23

Even so the tongue is a little member and boasts great things.
See how great a forest a little fire kindles!
James 3:5

It's early morning, and I awake to the sound of someone smacking his lips. What? Lip-smacking? I open my eyes to find Bandit standing over me staring me in the face. He has the all-too-familiar "I've got a problem" look on his face, and he is opening and closing his mouth making a sound like someone smacking his lips. As my head clears of the sleep cobwebs, it occurs to me that Bandit seems to be trying to control an excess of saliva. Then it dawns on me. He has to *vomit!*. He does this whenever he has to vomit. There's this very short "warning period" when he seems to be dealing with too much saliva, and then out comes the vomit. I'm wide awake now! I grab him and race for the back door and put him down in the grass. He retches painfully and out it comes—bright yellow, icky stomach bile. It's early morning, and he hasn't eaten since the night before, so there's nothing in his stomach to bring up—except bile.

Some mornings I'm not this lucky. Those mornings I awake to the sound of Bandit retching in the living room or on the floor near my bed. I jump from bed, but it's too late. The rug sports a glaring yellow spot. Luckily, I've discovered a cleaner that will get the spot out of the rug, but it's a hassle—to say the least.

Except for vomit, Bandit has complete control of his bodily emissions. He never has an "accident" in the house. Our rug has no pee-pee or poo-poo smells or stains, but it has more than its share of vomit rings. The cleaner gets the stain out, but there remains a "ghost" of where it was.

I'm reminded of my own besetting sin—contentious, uncontrollable mouth! Most of my friends think of me as a kind, caring person. Ask them, and they will tell you. They don't *live* with me, however. The person who is with me day in and day out could tell you a different story. My poor husband, Jim, gets the brunt of my every frustration. I try to control my tongue, but it has a mind of its own. Words fly out of my mouth without so much as a passing nod at my brain—mean, vindictive words—words intended to hurt and maim. They hit their target, Jim's beleaguered psyche, and he reacts with stony silence. It's a pattern we developed early in our marriage, and—I'm embarrassed to say—it continues to this day.

I've talked to the Lord about this often. I've repented in spiritual "sackcloth and ashes"—not only to the Lord, but to Jim as well. Jim accepts my apologies, but the damage is done. I have vomited out my anger, and although I've done my best to clean up the fallout, there remains the ghost ring on the rug of Jim's spirit—witness to the words I've projectile vomited on him. Words can never be retrieved. They have been spoken, they have hit their mark, and they have left an indelible imprint.

This is a second marriage for Jim and me. We made up our minds very early on that we were going to stick together, no matter what. We were not going to fail at marriage—again. We are both just stubborn enough to make good on this vow. So we have developed a "dance" that we do in order to keep our marriage's equilibrium. When I spew belligerent words, Jim clams up and says nothing. When I berate him for not talking with me and sharing his feelings, he points out that the environment is unsafe for such expressions. Sadly, he is correct.

On the rare occasions when he has attempted to explain his side of an argument, I have come back at him with more compelling arguments for *my* side of the incident. So he has learned that it's futile to argue back. His only recourse is to remain silent and let me regurgitate my acrimony. I could go into long excuses of having grown up in a household with a domineering mother and a passive father and how that environment shaped who I am today. But the truth is that I have no one to blame but myself. My sister grew up in the same environment, and she isn't a sharp-tongued shrew. *I* am the shrew.

Just as Bandit has no control of the vomit that spews from his mouth, I seem to lack control of the words that disgorge from mine. I don't scold him for vomiting because I know he has no control over it. It occurs to me that Lord doesn't scold me for my lack of control, either. My own conscience chastens me, but the Lord doesn't. I've come to Him contrite and I've gone to Jim contrite and asked for forgiveness. Forgiveness has come readily from the Lord and from Jim. Neither has ever chastised me. I've asked the Lord to set a watch over my tongue. I've asked Him to stop the words before they ever get to my lips. But I sometimes picture Him throwing His divine hands into the air and exclaiming, "How can I set a watch to stop words in your brain when your words never pass through it?"

Jim and I recently visited with Sylvia and Matt in their home in Macon, Georgia. My great-niece, Kelly, came over and brought her Chihuahua, Bambi. Bambi probably doesn't weigh more than four pounds. When Kelly brought her in the back door, and Bambi saw Bandit standing there, she was all teeth and snarls. At first, Bandit gave it right back to her, but then he did a very odd thing for him. He stopped barking back at her, and he *cowered!*

I have never seen Bandit afraid of or cowering before another dog, and as explained in a later chapter, I have no doubt that he would stand up to one of our Florida alligators or bob-cats. He will take on any *thing*, any *size*. He is not the least bit afraid of Shiloh a *huge* German Shepherd who lives in our neighborhood. When we are out for a walk and Bandit spots Shiloh, he literally *lunges* at the big brute. And Shiloh lunges back. They shout doggy insults at each other and strain against their leashes while Shiloh's owner and I desperately drag them in opposite directions. Bandit is definitely secure in his alpha dog manhood!

Bambi was another story, however. Bandit didn't assert his alpha disposition against Bambi. She consistently came at him firing a barrage of indictments, and Bandit *caved*. He just caved. She knew how to push his buttons, and he cowered in the wake of her onslaught. He spent most of the evening with his back turned to Bambi and his head and tail down in a submissive posture. Or, he hid behind the sofa. I laughingly called Bambi "Devil Woman" and began singing some of the words to the Marty Robbins song of the same name. Everyone laughed that anything as pint-sized as Bambi could possibly be dubbed a "Devil Woman." But she is. She is. Just ask Bandit!

I tried to think what the difference might be between Shiloh's abuses and Bambi's. I think Matt made the correct observation. He said that Bambi was female and small. Bandit knew instinctively that if he came against her, he could hurt her, and it wouldn't be right to hurt a female less than a third of his size. So, he opted for silence and submission.

The Lord gave me an insight as I watched Bambi's outrage against Bandit. Suddenly, I saw in Bambi and Bandit the "dance" that Jim and I play out from time to time. I saw me spewing out invectives and I saw that Jim *elects* to submit. I have thought him to be passive, but I realize that he isn't. He *chooses* to remain silent. I'm not the strong one; he is. He is strong enough not to rail back when railed against. That takes strength of character. I realize, sadly, that don't have that quality. I want it and I pray for it, but I don't have it—at least, not as of this writing. But I'm heartened to remember that I'm a work in progress, and God isn't finished with me yet.

I'm encouraged to know that He can reveal myself to

me in the behavior of a tiny Chihuahua raging against a much larger Shih Tzu. God *is* teaching me, and I hope (for Jim's sake) that I am learning.

I long to be like the virtuous wife of Proverbs 31, but I fall far short of that lofty goal. A counselor once explained to me that there's *no* woman like the one in Proverbs 31. He said that the Proverb describes a model to which to aspire, not something anyone has attained, or could attain. I hope he's right, for I don't see myself as ever being able to reach such perfection. Regardless, the virtuous woman is a wonderful role model, and I pray that God will grant me some of her graciousness. He well knows that, at this point, I severely lack most of it.

You may be wondering why I included this chapter admitting to my failed first marriage and my inadequacies in this marriage. I included it because I want you to understand that I have in no way attained to whatever God is shaping me to be. "Christians aren't perfect, just forgiven" is clearly true in my own experience. Jesus Christ and the Proverbs 31 woman are quintessential examples of a perfection to which I will *never* even come close.

Perhaps you struggle with issues of your own, and maybe you are striving to be better than you are. Self-improvement is a worthwhile pursuit, but I encourage you to let God mold you. Rest in the fact that He "Leads His Dear

Children Along," just as the words to the old hymn assure us: *Some through the water, some through the flood, some through the fire, but all through the blood*—the blood of the dear Savior who died for us, so that we don't have to be perfect, just forgiven.

Who can find a virtuous wife?
For her worth is far above rubies.
The heart of her husband safely trusts her;
So he will have no lack of gain.
She does him good and not evil
All the days of her life.

She seeks wool and flax,
And willingly works with her hands.
She is like the merchant ships,
She brings her food from afar.
She also rises while it is yet night,
And provides food for her household,
And a portion for her maidservants.

She considers a field and buys it;
From her profits she plants a vineyard.
She girds herself with strength,
And strengthens her arms.
She perceives that her merchandise is good,
And her lamp does not go out by night.
She stretches out her hands to the distaff,
And her hand holds the spindle.

She extends her hand to the poor,
Yes, she reaches out her hands to the needy.
She is not afraid of snow for her household,
For all her household is clothed with scarlet.
She makes tapestry for herself;
Her clothing is fine linen and purple.

Her husband is known in the gates,
When he sits among the elders of the land.
She makes linen garments and sells them,
And supplies sashes for the merchants.
Strength and honor are her clothing;
She shall rejoice in time to come.

She opens her mouth with wisdom,
And on her tongue is the law of kindness.
She watches over the ways of her household,
And does not eat the bread of idleness.

Her children rise up and call her blessed;
Her husband also, and he praises her:
"Many daughters have done well,
But you excel them all."

Charm is deceitful and beauty is passing,
But a woman who fears the Lord, she shall be praised.
Give her of the fruit of her hands,
And let her own works praise her in the gates.
Proverbs 31:10-31

Chapter Thirteen
The God of All Comfort

Let, I pray, Your merciful kindness be for my comfort,
According to Your word to Your servant.
Let Your tender mercies come to me, that I may live;
For Your law is my delight.
Psalm 119:76-77

Blessed be the God and Father of our Lord Jesus Christ,
the Father of mercies and God of all comfort,
who comforts us in all our tribulation,
that we may be able to comfort those who are in any trouble,
with the comfort with which we ourselves are comforted by God.
2 Cor.1:3-4

And I will pray the Father,
and he shall give you another Comforter,
that he may abide with you for ever . . . .
John 14:16 (KJV)

But the Comforter, which is the Holy Ghost,
whom the Father will send in my name,
he shall teach you all things,
and bring all things to your remembrance,
whatsoever I have said unto you.
John 14:26 (KJV)

Blessed are they that mourn; for they shall be comforted.
Matthew 5:4 (KJV)

I am sick. I'm lying in the bed sick! It's mid-August, and I have a summer cold. It's a hot, sultry day in Florida—the kind of day where you hate to leave your car in the sun because you know you will get third degree burns from the steering wheel when you return. There's no way I would own a car with leather seats in Florida! Unfortunately, I had to be out of the house this morning. Meals do not take into account that the meal preparer is sick. So I had made a dutiful trip to the grocery store. Actually, I felt pretty good earlier today and thought that maybe I had dodged a real doozy of a cold or flu.

That was this morning. This is now. Now I have a backache—which I always get when I have a fever. I have a sore throat. My sinuses are clogged; yet my nose is runny. How can my head be stuffed up and yet my nose run? If everything in my head is solidified, where does the runny stuff come from? I'm sneezing. I have a mild headache. And my entire body just feels "dull." I feel as if all my "shine" has gone.

I need comfort; I need someone to say "poor baby." I need someone to just love on me. Ever feel that way? Are you the type of person, like me, who needs someone around you when you are sick or distraught? Or, are you like my husband, who just wants to be left alone. Jim does not need or want any "poor baby" commiserations. When he is sick, he simply wants to be left alone. Whether he lives or dies, he doesn't want any fussing over him.

I think Jim is unusual in this, though. I feel certain that most people enjoy having some empathy and consolation when sick or in pain or otherwise troubled.

I'm thinking about comfort today as I lie sick in bed. I'm thinking about how God ministers to our needs in unexpected ways. Bandit has been sitting on my bed as I have sniffled, sneezed, blown and coughed, and as I have bemoaned my inflamed throat and aching body. He has been there for a while now, having come into my room and apparently sensed that not all was well with me. Recently, I have been reading Cesar Millan's book *Cesar's Way*,[5] and he says that dogs can sense a person's energy level. I'm thinking Bandit is sensing that mine is pretty low. He crawls up beside me, lays his head on my shoulder and looks at me with doleful eyes. Since he is such an alpha dog, he looks right into my eyes. He doesn't back down from a stare! But this time it isn't a challenging stare; it's a "what's wrong?" gaze. He knows that things are not right.

He gathers himself close to me and renders what comfort he can. This simple act of doggy kindness started me thinking about God's comfort in times of illness and trouble. Bandit just "came along side" me that way the Holy Spirit, the "Comforter"does. He lay there for a while assessing the situation and simply offering consolation. After a time, he decided that things were okay, *i.e.,* I wasn't going to die right away—although I feel like disputing that assessment at the moment—and he dropped off to sleep lying beside me.

I'm reminded of my friend Kathy and how she, too, came along side me in a time of trouble. I met Kathy when she and her husband moved to Florida shortly after the death of their beautiful son Anthony from AIDS. Kathy is one of the kindest most sympathetic souls I have ever encountered. She epitomizes 2 Corinthians 1:4b: . . . *that we may be able to comfort them which are in any trouble, by the comfort wherewith we ourselves are comforted of God.* The great sorrow that Kathy endured has given her extraordinary sympathy for others who are grieving, and she is able to give such tremendous comfort because she has experienced such immense loss.

When my mother and stepfather were dying in a nursing home, Kathy was my angel. You may have seen the email that circulated a while ago which says something to the effect that "Friends are like angels who lift us to our feet when our wings have trouble remembering how to fly." My friend Jan puts a small ornament on her Christmas tree each year. It's a figure of a hobo. She calls it an "angel unawares"—referring to Hebrews 13:2, *Be not forgetful to entertain strangers: for thereby some have entertained angels unawares.* (KJV). Kathy was my "angel unawares."

She would show up at my front door, or slip quietly up onto my porch when she happened to see me sitting there, and simply offer friendship and compassion. Late one afternoon, a few days after my mother had died, I found myself walking resolutely toward Kathy's house. My heart was heavy, and the sinking sun seemed to darken my mood unbearably. I felt drawn to Kathy, and I headed for her house. She met me at her front door with tears in her eyes. She just *knew*. She held out her arms, embraced me without a word, and we cried together. Then she went into her kitchen and made tea. We sat for a long time in her living room, talking, drinking tea, watching the sun go down, and the night sky appear. It must have been around nine that evening before I finally went home—my heart lighter, my mood lifted by the sheer magnitude of Kathy's compassion.

It's been five years since that day, but I recently thanked Kathy again for being there for me. I told her to take comfort in the fact that her son's death was not in vain—that her sweet, quiet, loving spirit had emerged from the ashes of that terrible pain. I cannot imagine a pain worse than losing a child. No parent should ever outlive his or her child. Yet, the "God of all comfort" can comfort us even through something that terrible and then turn it into consolation for others. Kathy's sweet spirit is living testimony that this is true.

As I continued to think about misery and comfort, my mind turned to Paul and his valedictory as he wrote to Timothy from a Roman prison. He asked Timothy to come to him and to come quickly.

> *Be diligent to come to me quickly; for Demas has forsaken me, having loved this present world, and has departed for Thessalonica—Crescens for Galatia, Titus for Dalmatia. Only Luke is with me. Get Mark and bring him with you, for he is useful to me for ministry. And Tychicus I have sent to Ephesus. Bring the cloak that I left with Carpus at Troas when you come—and the books, especially the parchments.... At my first defense no one stood with me, but all forsook me. May it not be charged against them.* 2 Timothy 4:9-13, 16

Alone and in prison, Paul was asking for three kinds of comfort: The comfort of Timothy's fellowship, the comfort of warm clothing, and the comfort of the word of God. Having been abandoned by friends and fellow believers and co-workers in the ministry, he sits alone in a cold, damp dungeon and needs the warmth of human fellowship. But notice that he particularly wants the parchments! The Bible does not explain what the parchments were. Some scholars think they might have been scripture and/or copies of Paul's previous epistles. Whatever they were, Paul's need for physical comfort seems secondary to his need for emotional and spiritual comfort. He needs the physical comfort of the warm cloak, but he *accentuates* his need for the emotional and spiritual comfort of Christian fellowship and of God's word.

I am heartened today as I reminisce about Kathy and about Paul's message in Second Timothy. But I have no Christian fellowship at the moment—no milk of human kindness. I have only Bandit's fellowship. Jim is away from home and not expected to return for several hours. When he left this morning, I was in much better shape than I am right now. Jim knows how I need that "poor baby" consolation when I'm sick. So if he knew how awful I'm feeling at the moment, he would come home. I resist the temptation to call him on his cell phone and bemoan my plight.

I am grateful for Bandit's comfort, and I told him so. I told him that he was a "good boy" which usually means he is going to get a treat—a "Buddy Biscuit." He perked up immediately, and since I couldn't bear to disappoint him, I dragged myself out of bed and went to the kitchen and got the doggy biscuit. He has long since devoured it and now again sits happily by my side chewing a chew stick, which he found on the way back to the bedroom after finishing off the Buddy Biscuit.

Instead of concentrating on my cold and how miserable I feel right now, I'm just intensely grateful for the astounding truth that the God of the Universe takes notice when one of His children is grieved, or not feeling well, and sends comfort and compassion. I think I also learned something today about being grateful for comfort—as in the reward I gave Bandit for his faithfulness. Obviously, I wouldn't offer God a Buddy Biscuit, but I do offer Him my profound gratitude for His provision of comfort—especially for the comfort He sent through Kathy when I had such a broken heart five years ago, and for the comfort He sent today in the form of a small dog.

Chapter Fourteen
Fear and Trust

What time I am afraid, I will trust in Thee.
Psalm 56:3 (KJV)

The LORD is my light and my salvation; Whom shall I fear?
The LORD is the strength of my life; Of whom shall I be afraid?
Psalm 27:1

He who dwells in the shelter of the Most High
Will abide in the shadow of the Almighty.
I will say to the LORD, My refuge and my
fortress, My God, in whom I trust
Psalm 91:1-2 (NASB)

I am sitting in my chair trying to read. Suddenly I have the feeling that I'm being watched. I look up and there is Bandit, staring at me. He has that look in his eyes—fear! Then I realize that way off in the distance there is a soft rumble of thunder. We get lots of thunderstorms in Florida, and Bandit is intensely afraid of thunder. He doesn't like any loud or strange noise, but he is particularly fearful of thunder. He jumps into my lap and starts to tremble all over. He will keep this up until the storm passes. He comes to me for comfort, yet he won't let me comfort him. When I try to hold him, he pulls away and suspiciously eyes the outside through the glass doors of the family room. He is anxiously awaiting the next thunder boom! He knows instinctively that these early warning soft rumblings in the distance are the harbinger of the loud crashes to come. With each sound, his trembling and anxiety become more pronounced. I may have to resort to "doggy beer."

Doggy beer is the term coined by the employees of a pet supply store I frequent. It's chicken jerky strips with some calming agents infused—the main one being hops. That's right, hops—just as in beer. Unfortunately, it doesn't even touch the kind of fear that thunder engenders in Bandit. Even after a doggy beer, Bandit will continue to tremble and pace and jump in and out of my lap and climb up me, until the thunderstorm has passed. I don't know why thunder causes Bandit to climb, but he will climb anything in sight. I once came home to find him on the kitchen counter. Bandit is less than a foot tall, so at first I was completely at a loss as to how he got up on a thirty-six-inch high kitchen counter top. Then I remembered that we had a thunderstorm while I was out. We have two recliner chairs in our family room adjacent to the kitchen. The backs of the recliners are tall and are relatively close to the breakfast bar that is joined to the kitchen counter. The breakfast bar is actually forty-two inches high—six inches higher than the counter top.

I know that Bandit often climbs on those chairs and up the back whenever he hears thunder. So I realized that, driven by fear, he had leapt from the back of one of the chairs and onto the breakfast bar and then down onto the counter. Once there, he was smart enough to realize he would hurt himself if he tried to jump down, so he was stuck until I got home. I don't understand why he heads for "higher ground" when he hears thunder. Maybe he realizes that thunder accompanies rain, and floods can sometimes be the result of rain. He has never actually been in a flood, but maybe there's some instinct in him that knows of the possibility of floods. Whatever it is, Bandit wants *up* when the rains come down.

On the other hand, he climbs at the veterinarian's office as well. I try to sit quietly and hold him, and he climbs right up the front of me and attempts to get up onto my shoulders. Obviously, there's no danger of flooding when we are there on a bright, sunny Florida day. So it must be simply fear of the unknown that drives this tiny creature to seek to be "taller" on a higher plane.

Bandit displays an odd sort of "trust" in me and my abilities to "save" him from whatever the immediate distress. It's the same kind of "trust" I often exhibit toward God. Whenever something frightens my little pooch, he will leap into my lap for reassurance. But then he does not rest in my strength or allow me to comfort him. Whether it's thunder, or firecrackers, or vet visits, or whatever the perceived danger, Bandit follows the same pattern. He jumps into my lap, stares at me with hopeful, trusting eyes, and then proceeds to tremble and pump his little feet up and down. Then he starts climbing for higher ground—right up the front of me! He wants to trust, but he can't. The fear is too intense, the "danger" too threatening. He can't relax and enjoy my protection and the doggy beer! By the way, after the thunderstorm has passed and Bandit's fear subsides, then the doggy beer kicks in and he gets a nice nap!

I have had trust issues with God for as long as I can remember. In fact, I feel certain that what trials I have had in life have been for the sole purpose of teaching me to trust Him. Yet, I don't—but then I do—and then I don't again. Can I get a witness here? I do know this: Whenever I have been able to let go and let God—as the platitude goes—He has *always* come through. He is totally trustworthy. He never fails. He is faithful. So why do I continue to fight this battle?

Once the thunderstorm subsides and things get back to normal, Bandit brings a toy to me, and I throw it into the living room. He runs after it and brings it back to me. At first, he drops the toy at my feet, and it seems as though he is going to give it to me so that I can throw it again, and the game continue.

But, alas, just as I reach for it, he quickly snaps it up again. I can't pull it from his clenched teeth. He has a death grip on it. He brings me his toy as if he *wants* to surrender it, but he won't *let go*. He never quite understands that it's the *letting go* that gives me the ability to throw the toy again and bring him joy. No matter how often I throw the toy, Bandit never quite trusts me enough to give it to me. I have to wrestle it away from him or trick him into releasing it.

It occurred to me that I usually do the same thing whenever I have a problem. I bring it to the Lord, He removes it from me (*as far as the East is from the West*, Psalm 103:12), but I go searching for it and take it up again. I bring the problem back to the Lord for Him to remove it again, and just as He reaches for it, I snatch it up, growling. "Leave my problem alone! I can handle this one myself! Grrrr." So God releases it back into my custody. And then what? I'm stuck with a useless problem again. It's no good—the game is no good, nothing happens—unless I release it.

At last, Bandit gets bored with the game, and he just lets the toy lie wherever I throw it. He is at peace; he doesn't need to take it up again. He's done with the game. He drifts off to sleep.

Will I ever learn to be done with the game? Will I ever learn to trust and rest?

Chapter Fifteen

Freedom!

If you abide in My word, you are My disciples indeed.
And you shall know the truth, and the truth shall make you free.
John 8:31b-32

And Jesus said to them,
"I am the bread of life.
He who comes to Me shall never hunger,
and he who believes in Me shall never thirst."
John 6:35

Jesus answered and said to her,
"If you knew the gift of God,
and who it is who says to you, 'Give Me a drink,'
you would have asked Him,
and He would have given you living water."
John 4:10

As I pulled my car into the driveway one bright, sunny summer afternoon not long ago, I was astonished to see Bandit sitting outside in the grass under the oak trees in our front yard. Jim's van was missing from the driveway, so I knew that no one was at home—no one, that is, except *Bandit*. I could hardly believe my eyes. How had he gotten outside, and why was he casually lazing around under the trees enjoying the summer breeze? He had newfound freedom! Why hadn't he run away?

Bandit's being outside alone is more of a concern than you might think at first blush. Here are the alarming facts: Almost every pond, large or small, in Florida has at least one resident alligator, and there is a small pond right across the street from our house. In all likelihood, a gator visits it from time to time. And there is a large bobcat who makes his habitat in the preserve behind our house. If Bandit (the exceptionally alpha dog) ever laid eyes on either of these beasts, he would most certainly take the brute on. And, no doubt, Bandit would lose!

We have seen the bobcat several times over the past two years, but he (she?) was always at some distance out in the preserve. Since bobcats are nocturnal animals, the times we have spotted him have always been in the early morning when he was most likely returning home from a night's prowl. It's uncharacteristic for a bobcat to be out much past sunrise. Nevertheless, I saw him up close and personal a few weeks ago at the uncommonly late hour of 8:30 in the morning.

The back of our house is almost entirely glass. Across the back are three large sliding glass doors in the family room, an aquarium type window in the breakfast nook, sliding glass doors in the living room, and sliding glass doors in our bedroom. All these doors and the window look out onto a sizable preserve.

I happened to be standing in the family room that particular morning when, much to my amazement, the bobcat sauntered out of the preserve and into our back yard. He strolled leisurely across our yard as if he didn't have a care in the world. Then he walked between our house and the neighbor's house to the west, stopping a couple of times to sniff at the neighbor's shrubbery near the bird feeder. He may have been hoping for a hapless bird as a late breakfast. The bobcat continued his trek, crossing the street in front of our house, casually circling the pond and then disappearing into the preserve on that side of the road. I was so flabbergasted that I didn't even think to grab a camera. I did, however, manage to yell to Jim, who was in our bedroom, "Quick, look out the window!"

I estimated the bobcat to be sixty or seventy pounds, but Jim says I misjudged. He thinks the cat was around forty pounds. I briefly researched bobcats on the Internet, and apparently Jim is right. Most websites describe the maximum weight of these felines at about forty pounds. This one looked larger than that to me, but since it's not often that one sees a large, wild cat meandering across one's lawn, one might tend to magnify its size. Regardless, he was magnificent! I felt singularly blessed for having witnessed this regal animal's solitary journey from preserve to preserve.

Then I recollected in horror the many mornings I have allowed Bandit to be outside unleashed for a few brief moments. In my mind's eye, I could see Bandit spotting the bobcat and going on the attack, and I could imagine the grim results.

Consequently, when I saw Bandit sitting contentedly under the oak trees alone in our front yard, with no one at home, my mind went to alligators and bobcats, and I was more than a little distressed. I was grateful that Bandit had possessed the common sense to stay in the yard rather than venturing into the preserves or over to the pond. A house cat belonging to our neighbors who live three houses west of us had slipped unnoticed out of their screened lanai one day several months ago and wandered into the preserve. Sadly, they discovered its mostly devoured body a few days later when they noticed buzzards circling near the edge of the preserve. I was horrified that Bandit could have wandered off and suffered a similar fate. But strangely he didn't use his freedom as license to run away.

In his remarkable book *Growing in Grace*,[6] Bob George describes our freedom in Christ by contrasting a city dog and a country dog. A city dog, always kept inside or penned or tied, will most likely bolt through an open door or open gate. In actuality though, he isn't running from his master; he loves his master. He is running from *bondage*. Likewise, a Christian bound in religious legalism, might bolt into sin when he first comes to the realization of the freedom we have in *grace*. As the newly freed Christian grows in grace, however, he comes to be like the country dog. The country dog, having all the freedom in the world—acres of fields, miles of forests—hangs around the house and sleeps on the front porch. Why? Because he loves his master and wants to please him and be near him. He awaits the moment his master will want to play or take him for a hike in the woods.

George goes on to explain that in the same way, as we mature in the freedom we have in grace, we want to stay close to the Lord and will not use our liberty as a license to sin.

> Why does the country dog stay near the front door when he has miles of freedom? Because he knows and loves his master. His freedom is not freedom *from* bondage, but freedom to be *with* the one he loves. In the same way, as I grow to know and love Jesus Christ more intimately I find myself experiencing incredible freedom and hardly think about the law at all. The issue is not what I *can* or *cannot* do. I am free to know my heavenly Father in an unhindered personal relationship. That's what I concentrate on. Then through that relationship God teaches my mind to think His thoughts. Where I am wrong, he reasons with me. He doesn't lock me back behind the fence!

Bandit is most definitely a city dog. He is seldom out of the house without a leash. Yet, when a door is opened, he doesn't bolt for freedom, and he didn't run away the day he was unwittingly given his freedom. Apparently, he has already developed such a love for Jim and me that he does not want to stray when given the opportunity. It turns out that, hoping to go for a ride, Bandit must have wandered out while Jim was loading some equipment into his van. Jim didn't notice him and drove off leaving him in the front yard.

It occurred to me that there are other compelling reasons that Bandit, a city dog, merely sat in the grass patiently waiting for someone to come home and let him back in the house. He was staying near the place where he *gets fed*. So I think the analogy goes even further than the fact that this dog knows and loves his master. He also knows that his master feeds him. Bandit was staying close to his food source!

I know and love Jesus Christ, and I am certain of His love for me. But He also *feeds* me. He is my bread of life and the conduit through whom flows living water directly from the Father to me. Why would I run away? As for me, I want to stay close to the source of my spiritual nourishment. I bask in those dazzling moments when I glean a nugget of truth from His word that I never noticed before or when I hear a learned and gifted preacher exposit a passage of scripture. When this happens, I feel spiritually fed.

I think *security* is another reason Bandit stayed put. When Bandit found himself locked out of the house that day, he simply was not daring enough to wander off. He wanted to stay where he feels secure.

In the same way, we feel secure when we make our dwelling place with the Lord and stay close to Him.

He who dwells in the secret place of the Most High
Shall abide under the shadow of the Almighty.

I will say of the LORD, "He is my refuge and my fortress;
My God, in Him I will trust."

Surely He shall deliver you from the snare of the fowler
And from the perilous pestilence.
Psalm 91:1-3

134

Chapter Sixteen
Christmas

And the Word was made flesh and dwelt among us.
And we beheld His glory,
the glory of the Only Begotten of the Father,
full of grace and truth.
John 1:14 (KJV)

It's December 2, and Jim and I are out riding our bicycles through the neighborhood and exulting in the warm sunshine. Warm Christmases are one of the many perks of living in Florida! The temperature is predicted to be in the mid eighties today—unseasonably warm, even for Florida. I can remember my first few Christmases here and how peculiar it seemed to walk past the Christmas tree while attired in a wet bathing suit—having just returned from the beach or just gotten out of the pool.

As we ride along today, many of the neighbors are outside stringing lights on their homes and shrubbery in celebration of the glorious advent—the birth of the Savior of the

135

world, the Messiah of Israel. I began reminiscing about Christmases past. I thought about Daddy and how he loved Christmas—how he delighted in decorating our modest home and yard.

It never occurred to me during my youth, but sometime during my adulthood, it dawned on me that our family had been poor. Daddy made do with whatever he could come up with for Christmas decorations. Our house had two picture windows in front—one in the living room and one in the dining room. Daddy strung really pitiful lights around those windows. Somewhere he had acquired two decidedly awful-looking strings of lights that would just fit around the picture windows. The light-strings were fitted for regular-sized bulbs—not Christmas type smaller ones. Since colored bulbs were an expense we didn't need, Daddy decided to paint plain old white light bulbs. He had a supply of tempera pigments, because he often painted signs to hang in the meat market where he worked. He created exceptionally artistic signs announcing such things as: "Whole Fryers! 29¢ lb.!" I would often sit on the floor with him in the living room as he painted on long rolls of white paper.

He had bright blue, red and green tempera "dust" that, when mixed with water, produced paint for the signs. So he mixed several batches and coated the light bulbs in bright hues. The only problem was . . . . Well, actually, there were a number of problems. Everything from ancient, disintegrating, and I suspect downright dangerous wires (intended for indoors, but presently outside in the weather), to toasted paint smoldering on extremely hot lights. After only a few hours, the bright colors were reduced to burnt umber. Yet, a little of the intended colors still shone bravely through, so the lights remained around the windows.

At some point, around middle age, I had eventually become aware of our family's poverty as I mused one day about the two Christmas trees Daddy always put up—one for each picture window. It had never occurred to me before to wonder why Daddy had invariably waited until the last minute to put up the trees. I had regularly started begging for the trees almost immediately after Thanksgiving. But Daddy would put me off, promising faithfully to bring home the trees "soon." Then, finally, a day or so before Christmas, "soon" abruptly arrived, and Daddy would come home with two trees tied to the top of the car.

The grocery store where he worked sold Christmas trees—aromatic blue spruce lined up on the sidewalk along the storefront. To this day, a real Christmas tree to me is a live blue spruce. All the others are just wannabes. It was only as an adult that I came to realize that Daddy had been waiting for the trees to go on sale just before Christmas because prior to then, they were just too expensive. I suspect that employees were allowed to get their own trees for free at that point. Our trees were inevitably a scraggly lot—undesirable leftovers because of a hole in the shape or some other glaring defect. Regardless, we camouflaged the flaw with decorations and icicles—you know, the shiny, silvery ones. We always used lots of icicles to make up for the fact that we had few decorations. We barely had enough ornaments to adequately cover one medium-sized tree—let alone two rather large ones.

My sister and I routinely got into a squabble over the icicles. Sylvia was much more interested in having a beautiful tree, while I was just into the fun of decorating. She insisted that we carefully position each and every icicle to its maximum resplendence. I would start out obediently making sure that I placed every icicle just so. But, after a box or two of the stringy things, I would start tossing them haphazardly onto the tree—partly in sheer exuberance and partly because real splendor just takes too long to achieve.

Although we always had the extra tree in the dining room picture window, the living room tree was the main attraction. It received the most attention and the lion's share of our meager decorations. It was under the living room tree that Santa would leave our presents. I supposed that it was because of it's proximity to the chimney. After all, Santa had lots of places to go on Christmas Eve, so any steps he could save would be significant.

On Christmas morning, we would awaken to the heady aroma of oranges and apples. Daddy always put lots of oranges and apples and nuts under the tree, probably to disguise the shortage of presents. Don't get me wrong. We never felt deprived in any way. Somehow, Santa invariably managed to bring the items that were our hearts' desires—with a few extra treasures thrown in for good measure.

Christmas was a magical time in our little town. The main streets through Fitzgerald are divided with medians, which everyone called "parks," separating north/south and east/west traffic. There were decorations downtown and on all the medians. A local artist, Inez Archer, painted figures cut out from plywood, and they were erected on the medians and illuminated by flood lights. There were snowmen, Santa Clauses, Christmas trees, angels, the Holy Family, shepherds, sheep—the whole Christmas experience artistically recreated in plywood.

One of the local churches had a Christmas pageant that rivals in my mind any professional theater presentation I have ever seen. Apparently, the church was underfunded so that adequate heat was a luxury. I remember that it was always so cold that I thought my feet would freeze before the performance ended. The nativity was played out with local businessmen dressed in robes as wise men, shepherds and Joseph. A beautiful raven-haired woman, named Irene Livingston, played the part of Mary. With a sweet, demure countenance, she was perfect for the part.

And I'm confident that there has never been a more convincing wise man than Elmer Archer, the local barber, and the artist Inez's husband. The three wise men tramped down the aisle singing "We Three Kings." Each wise man sang the verse about the particular gift he brought, and then they all joined together on the chorus:

> *Oh-oh, star of wonder, star of night,*
> *Star with royal beauty bright.*
> *Westward leading, still proceeding,*
> *Guide us to thy perfect light.*

For a cigar smoker, Elmer had an exceptionally good voice. I remember its clarity as he sang about the myrrh he brought:

> *Myrrh is mine, its bitter perfume,*
> *Breathes a life of gathering gloom.*
> *Sorrowing, sighing, bleeding, dying,*
> *Sealed in a stone-cold tomb.*

These were disturbingly somber, haunting, confusing and frightening words to my young ears as I sat in the darkened, stone-cold church—the only lights being the floods illuminating the make-shift stage.

White sheets served as curtains to close off the "stage" between acts. Act I was the announcement to Mary, Joseph's dream, and their later journey to Bethlehem. Act II was the scene at the inn and in the stable culminating in the arrival of the Christ child. Act III was the announcement to the "shepherds abiding in the fields." Act IV was the arrival of the shepherds and the wise men with their gifts.

My sister was the heralding angel who sang to the shepherds. She was up in the darkened balcony, a single flood light trained on her. She wore a white robe, wings and a halo and seemed to glow as the bright light cast her in stark relief against the darkness behind her. The hymn she sang is titled "How Great Our Joy." A choir of less-important (in my childish mind) angels on the platform below would sing the chorus, and my sister would echo from the balcony above.

Choir: How great our joy.
Echo: Great our joy.
Choir: Joy, joy, joy.
Echo: Joy, joy, joy.
Choir: Glory to God in heaven on high.
Echo: Glory to God in heaven on high.

I was so proud of my sister, and she looked so beautiful up there in the balcony. I thought she looked just like an angel. I longed for the day when I would get to play the part of the heralding angel. That day never came. They stopped having the pageant before I was old enough to play the part.

Santa would arrive each year with a parade. He rode on

one of the city fire trucks. Rumor was that he arrived by helicopter, was met at the tiny local airport by the firemen and brought into town on the truck. I invariably checked him out carefully to see if we had been lucky enough to get the "real" Santa or if, alas, we had been consigned one of his helpers in a wig and fake beard. From time to time, I concluded that we actually had Mr. Claus himself.

Even if we didn't get him in person in the parade, we always had him on the radio. He would read letters sent to him by the community children each year. I'm not sure exactly how all those letters made their way to Wade Malcolm, the dear heart who actually "Ho, Ho, Hoed" each year on the radio and carefully read each letter and promised to deliver the prized toys. But, somehow, the local post office cooperated or perhaps there were special boxes around town to receive the letters addressed simply to:

Santa Claus
North Pole

I was reminiscing over all these Christmas memories with Jim this morning as we rode along on our bikes and watched neighbors precariously perched on tall ladders carefully attaching lights to roof lines. I wondered aloud if there might be truly spectacular decorations and a marvelous celebration going on in Heaven every Christmas. "I doubt it," came the abrupt response from Jim, a Bible scholar and theological literalist. I'm sure his mind went immediately to the fact that Christ was not born in December, Christmas trees are from a pagan celebration, and yada, yada, yada. I didn't want to go there, so I fell silent.

I don't like putting God in a box. If He wants to have a Christmas celebration in Heaven in December when all earth is celebrating Christmas, I think He certainly has the freedom, the power and the authority to do so. I also understand Jim's viewpoint that we can't run roughshod over clear teachings of scripture. But I didn't want to be a Bible student today; I wanted to let my mind play with the idea that there just might be all types of decorating going on in Heaven at this very moment, and that Daddy just might be having a high old time decorating with lights that are not painted with tempera paints.

It's the Christmas season, and my heart longs for home—as I am certain many hearts around the globe yearn right along with me. For some of us, our eyes fill with tears when we hear the words to the popular song, *I'll Be Home for Christmas*. Our childhood homes are long gone or are now occupied by strangers, our parents are long dead, our families are scattered.

This is 2006, and I have not really decorated for Christmas since Daddy died in 1984. Because Daddy loved Christmas so, it seemed appropriate that as he lay dying, Christmas carols played softly on the radio in his room. Thank

God he was at home—in his own room—not in a nursing home as were my mother and stepfather in their last days. He went home to our Lord just after midnight as the new year arrived. Daddy had taught me the joy of Christmas, and somehow when he died, my Christmas joy died with him. With each ensuing year as Christmas approached, I often thought of decorating. Occasionally, I would hang a wreath or put some lights on a lamp post, but could never marshal the emotional strength to do any real decorating or put up a tree.

For the past four years, I have been rediscovering God's love. It is not a coincidence that Bandit has been with me for lo these last four years. He came into my life just about this time in 2002—early December. He was just eight weeks old, and so small that someone who saw him in my arms that day asked if he was a hamster. This tiny being covered in fur has brought a spiritual warmth into my life. God has used Bandit to bring about a softening of my heart. As a byproduct of the love I feel for Bandit and the love I feel coming back to me from him, the coldness of my spirit has begun an early spring thaw. For the first time in a very long time, my house is resplendent with Christmas decorations this year. Our house is up for sale, so this is probably the last year we will spend in a beautiful home that the Lord provided for us for a season. I don't know what He has in store for us, but I can trust that, whatever it is, it will work together for good.

Standing tall in our living room is a beautiful, seven-foot tree—loaned to us by a friend. It's artificial, so there's no blue spruce olfactory ecstasy, but there is the visual delight of graceful green boughs decorated with only white twinkle lights, red velvet bows and white snowflake ornaments I purchased at the dollar store—ten snowflakes for a dollar. It cost very little, but it looks beautiful and majestic. Thanks to our son, Alan, there are lighted artificial palm trees outside in the front gardens and lighted icicle lights dangling from the eaves. Just looking at the decorations fills me with joy, and I feel the closeness of my earthly Daddy's love and that of my Heavenly Father God.

Yet, my heart longs for home and that magical time when I believed that Santa actually squished himself down our tiny chimney and left wondrous gifts for me and my sister as we slept in our cozy beds on a frosty Christmas Eve.

Chapter Seventeen
God Bless You, Sweetheart

Be not forgetful to entertain strangers:
for thereby some have entertained angels unawares.
Hebrews 13:2 (KJV)

It was a cold January day in Florida. The weatherman had predicted that the night's temperatures would drop into the mid to low thirties. Brrr. Mighty chilly for Florida! I had just walked into the super market and had spied a grocery basket piled high with cozy dog crate liners made of acrylic fleece. I couldn't believe the low price—only $9.99! I had often thought of getting one of these for Bandit, but the cheapest I had seen them was *twice* that price. Because of our ever worsening financial condition following our sojourn as would-be real estate entrepreneurs, Jim and I had been trying our best to conserve money. But at half the price, this was just too good of an offer to pass up! I grabbed the fleecy prize without a moment's hesitation.

That's when he passed me and smiled. I sensed his presence an instant before I actually saw him. He was dirty and looked as though he was wearing all the clothes he owned. He was one of the homeless people who lived nearby. Some months previous, we had become aware of a colony of homeless citizenry living in a wooded area right next to the Publix we frequent. We often saw them walking along the sidewalk nearby or dotting the proximate intersections, with ever-present signs in their hands announcing the bearer's particular plight—homeless, hungry, willing to work for food.

Now, just as I tossed the warm doggy bunting into my basket, the homeless man—who would spend the long night freezing with little or no shelter—smiled at me and greeted me with a kindly "God bless you." The irony of our circumstances stunned and shamed me. My dog would spend the evening in our beautiful, warm house with all the comforts of home. The homeless stranger would spend the night shivering near a makeshift fire and praying for the warm morning sun. My dog was getting a cozy bed he didn't really need. In contrast, who knew whether the sensitive-faced man had even a blanket? Bandit sleeps snug and content in bed with Jim and me. Yet, I was about to spend ten dollars for a warm liner for his, mostly unused, crate.

The homeless man's "God bless you" pierced my heart. He didn't say it in an accusatory or unkind or sarcastic way. He said it sincerely and accompanied it with a beatific smile. He practically glowed with God's love. It warmed my soul. How ironic that I was so warmed by a sweet, kind being who would endure paralyzing cold himself the remainder of the night.

I wanted to fling the liner from my basket and rush after the man, plead his forgiveness for my callousness, and press ten dollars—no twenty—into his icy hand. But as quickly as he had appeared at my side, he had vanished out the door. I stood transfixed. . . and then I proceeded to do exactly what I would have done if I had never encountered the stranger. I continued my grocery shopping and went through the check out line with my groceries. . . and the dog crate liner. Although my conscience had weighed heavily on me as I traversed the aisles in the store, eventually the bargain price of the liner had won out. I bought it.

Several times since that evening, I have told friends the story of this shopping experience. I actually ran into a friend that very night in the grocery store, and I told her how conscience-stricken I felt about buying the liner. She, and all others who have since heard the story, have assured me that Bandit needs me to take care of him, and I shouldn't feel guilty about buying for him. After all, when one gets a pet, one takes on the responsibility to see that the pet is well cared for. But, wait a minute, just where should my priorities be? Isn't it more important to help a homeless person get a blanket than to help an already spoiled dog live an even more comfortable life? Is there really any other answer here, except the obvious?

In my mind, I have often gone back to that moment in the grocery story. I think it was one of those "windows of the soul" that Ken Gire describes in his book by the same title.[7] He describes the "windows" as *moments when God has touched our lives like a soft hand of morning sun reaching through our bedroom window, brushing over our eyes, and waking us to something eternal.* He goes on to explain:

> At some of these windows, what we see offers simply a moment of insight, making us slower to judge and quicker to show understanding. *At a few of them, though, what we see offers a word spoken to the very depths of who we are.* It may be a word to rouse us from sleep and ready us for our life's journey. It may be a word to warn us of a precipice or guide us to a place of rest. It may be a word telling us who we are and why we are here and what is required of us at this particular juncture of our journey. (Emphasis mine.)

I suspected that the purpose of this particular window into my own soul was indeed spoken into my very depths to show me who I am—and I didn't particularly like what I saw.

I have often considered whether I could have caught the homeless man as he hastened out the door and given him the money I eventually spent for the liner. After my momentary, guilt-induced paralysis, could I have willed my legs to run out the door and into the parking lot quickly enough to overtake him? Could I have found the man who had given me such a sweet benediction? He had moved quickly—almost as if he merely wanted to pronounce a blessing on me and hurry away. Was he an "angel unawares"? Had I missed a significant opportunity—never to be offered again?

Lately, Jim and I have been considering whether we have been a good investment for God. What kind of return does He get from His investment in us? Has He not showered us with blessings? And at what rate of return? Oh, we dutifully drop our offerings into the plate as it's passed, and we help with this or that charity, or we give to someone with a particular need. But these seem mere tokens compared to the vast deficit all around us. Perhaps we are as poor a return for God as the investment houses had been for us. Perhaps it's the lesson we are to learn from that experience. Give more; be a better investment ourselves.

So we determined that we should carefully and prayerfully look for places where we can give back more. It may seem odd that we chose this point, when we have a minuscule income, to make a commitment to give more. But we have felt led to do so, maybe as a challenge of our faith. When we see so little coming in, do we have the faith to give more?

I was again at Publix today, and as I drove out of the parking lot, I was thinking about where God would have me give some money. I had awakened this morning to a beautiful springtime day. It's April fifth, and the air is warm and breezy. It's what I call "porch weather." I joke that it's the few days a year that make living in Florida year around worthwhile. It's a time when we open windows and doors and let the gentle, fragrant breeze sweep the winter doldrums from the house. It's the short interval before the intensely hot, humid days of summer—days we will spend sequestered in air conditioned confines. Today, the sun is shining brightly, and the air is energizing. It's a day when I would love to go to the beach, but I had to go to the grocery store instead.

I turned left out of the parking lot and as I neared the intersection, I noticed one of the ever-present homeless sitting in front of a road sign on the median separating the four lanes of traffic. The light at the intersection was red. He held the typical sign telling of his predicament, but I trained my eyes away from him and did not read his brown cardboard declaration. However, I couldn't help seeing the words "homeless" and "broke" as I turned away.

Suddenly, I remembered that I actually had some money in my purse. I usually carry absolutely no cash. If anyone ever mugged me, they would most likely get only credit cards and credit card receipts. Sounds like I have a credit card problem, right? Wrong. Jim and I use the cards the same as cash, paying the full balance every month, so that interest never accrues. Our principle is simple: Don't ever spend more on a credit card than you can pay at the end of the month. When the bill comes, pay it in full. Once you start carrying a balance, it gets extremely expensive, incredibly fast.

So today when I realized I actually had some cash, it was an unusual state of affairs. I carefully moved my purse to the front floorboard and unzipped it to make sure I was, in fact, funded. I didn't want to get the poor fellow's hopes up only to discover that I had no money, after all. Instantly, I found a ten-dollar bill. As I pressed the control, and my window began to roll down, the man quickly clambered to his feet. He approached smiling amiably. Reaching for the currency, he said, "Thank you, sweetheart. You are so kind." He clutched the bill and shoved it into his pocket without checking it's denomination. It occurred to me that even the homeless have a sense of decorum. It would have been impolite to scrutinize the gift. The polite thing was to accept and acknowledge, regardless of the amount. As he turned to walk to his post, he paused and looked back and directly into my eyes. He said in a sweet, kind voice, "God bless you, sweetheart."

The radiant smile, the kindly "God bless you." It seemed so familiar. Was he my angel unawares? Was he the same man I had seen in the store that cold January night? He had the same gracious smile and offered the same benevolent blessing. Had God given me another opportunity? Was it merely a coincidence that the cash I happened to have that day was the same amount I had spent for the dog crate liner months earlier? I don't know.

Driving away, I suddenly began to cry, and then sob. For a few seconds, it was as though the Lord allowed me actually to feel the sweetness of the stranger's spirit, the hopelessness of his circumstances, and the despair in his heart. For a scant moment, it seemed I could feel the warmth that my small gesture had set ablaze in his heart. The warmth enveloped my spirit and flooded my eyes with tears.

"God bless you too, sweetheart."

Chapter Eighteen
To Know Him
And the Fellowship of His Sufferings

That I may know Him
and the power of His resurrection,
and the fellowship of His sufferings
Philippians 3:10

[T]hank you that in the hunger I have
known in the wilderness and in the
thorns and nails I have known in the
world, I have learned to feel something
of the pain you felt when you walked
this earth . . . and something of the
fellowship of your sufferings, an
intimacy with you I would have never
known apart from tears . . . .
Moments with the Savior[8]
Ken Gire

Philippians 3:10 has always frightened me. I *want* to know Him, but at what cost? Do I really *want* the fellowship of His *sufferings*? One thing I *do* know. There *is* a fellowship in suffering. The things I have experienced have given me a heart for others who suffer.

I can recall a number of years ago hearing our Christian friend Bill bemoan the fact that his elderly mother was having hallucinations and was rapidly becoming unable to care for herself. He was agonizing over her condition and the possibility of finding an assisted living facility for her. She was the independent sort who did not want to live with Bill and his wife Betty.

They were casting about in their minds as to what to do for this dear old saint who had always cared so deeply for them. She had constantly been a steady rock undergirding the family. She was "Nana" to all the grandchildren. Now she was failing mentally faster than physically. She didn't understand that she could no longer live alone. Except for the gravity of her condition, "alone" would have been an almost amusing term. For, in her own mind, she definitely wasn't alone. As her hallucinations worsened, she regularly saw "visitors" with whom she had long conversations.

I can remember that I made no connection with Bill and Betty's despair and dilemma. What was the big deal? Nana was no longer able to care for herself; they needed to find a clean, efficient, compassionate place for her to spend her last days. She would probably make friends of her own age and similar condition, and she would be—if not happy—then at least content. Why all the hand-wringing? In other words, I didn't have a clue.

My lesson, learned though the wrenching experience of placing my own parents in a nursing home, would not come until several years later. Now—after experiencing my own mother's and stepfather's grievous "incarceration"—now, I get it. I understand. And I feel a fellowship with Bill and Betty.

No human understands another's suffering, unless he/she has experienced the same kind of misery. God knows this, so when we need comfort, He usually sends another person to minister to us. Often our experience of *God's* love is through the *human* love and concern of someone God sends—just as He sent Timothy to Paul when Paul was in prison. Oddly enough, in my darkest hour God sent me not another person, but a dog. He sent me a small dog to hold, to love and to receive love from. And through this human/dog love relationship, God has taught me a great deal about the God/human love relationship.

In the usual course of events, however, it is other people—friends, relatives, brothers and sisters in Christ—who come to our aid. They empathize because they have endured similar griefs and losses. From our own suffering, we learn to help others. The God of all comfort is able to comfort others through us, His children, who have suffered great losses, great physical pain, great mental anguish. Only through suffering do we "fellowship" with others who likewise struggle.

Blessed be the God and Father of our Lord Jesus Christ, the Father of mercies and God of all comfort, who comforts us in all our tribulation, that we may be able to comfort those who are in any trouble, with the comfort with which we ourselves are comforted by God.
2 Cor.1:3-4

This morning, as I was thinking on these things, it occurred to me that I can now rejoice in my suffering because I know that every hardship, every trial, every heartache, every physical pain, every grief, every anxiety—everything in my life—has worked together to make me the person I am today. I know that I would be a less compassionate person had it not been for the suffering, and I would have no fellowship with others who suffer. The suffering is painful, but the fellowship is sweet.

It's been a long, six-year, journey from the time I took the sad ride with my parents from the assisted living facility in Port Charlotte to the nursing home in Bradenton. Even today, the journey is painful. My eyes fill with tears as I write this. But, today, I can rejoice in the work that the suffering brought about in my heart.

Whenever I see someone pushing a wheelchair, I identify with how hard it is to lift someone into a wheelchair. It's heavy lifting, my friend. When the disabled person is completely unable to stand or push, the lift is extremely physically demanding. Prior to my mother being in a wheelchair, I had never thought of how much physical strength it takes to hoist someone in and out of a chair. I had never thought of how emotionally draining it is to see a loved one in such condition day in and day out. Now I know. Now, I will never be the same. Now, I have a fellowship with every person I see pushing a wheelchair and also with the dear soul *in* that wheelchair. I know the suffering. I know how my mother cried because of pain in her back from sitting in a wheelchair in a nursing home. I know the distress of finding her in such pain and angrily demanding that she be put to bed—only to find out that she was just taken from bed where she had also been crying in pain and begging to be put in the chair.

Life is tough. The end of life is not pretty. But there is a fellowship among those of us who have watched a loved one die a slow death, who have stood helplessly by as someone we love remains suspended somewhere between life and death. I have a friend named Angela who is caring for her mother and stepfather right now in her home. She moved them here from Kentucky. I call Angela regularly just to give her someone to talk with who understands what she is experiencing.

I would like to say at this point that I am whole—that I have made the journey and have arrived back to a wholeness. But I can't say that. In fact, I will never be able to say it. A piece of who I am died with my parents—with my father, with my stepfather and then with my mother. That piece is gone and I can never recover it. But the hole it left is being filled by the joy of knowing that God is refining me as silver in a flame. I am reminded of an email that I've seen several times. It's a story by an unknown author titled "Refining Fire."

Some time ago, a few ladies met in a certain city for Bible study. While reading the third chapter of Malachi they came upon a remarkable expression in the third verse: "And He shall sit as a refiner and purifier of silver." The verse puzzled some of the women, and they wondered what this statement meant about the character and nature of God. One of them offered to investigate the process of refining silver and report to the group at their next Bible study.

That week, the woman called a silversmith and made an appointment to watch him at work. She didn't mention anything about the reason for her interest beyond her curiosity about the process of refining silver.

As she watched the silversmith, he held a piece of silver over the fire and let it heat up. He explained that in refining silver, one needed to hold the silver in the middle of the fire where the flames were hottest in order to burn away all the impurities. The woman thought about God holding us in such a hot spot; then she thought again about the verse: "He sits as a refiner and purifier of silver." She asked the silversmith if it was true that he had to sit there in front of the fire the whole time the silver was being refined.

The man answered that yes, he not only had to sit there holding the silver, but he also had to keep his eyes on the silver the entire time it was in the fire. If the silver was left a moment too long in the flames, it would be destroyed. The lady at once saw the beauty, and comfort too, of the expression, "He shall sit as a refiner and purifier of silver."

The woman was silent for a moment. Then she asked the silversmith, "How do you know when the silver is fully refined?"

He smiled at her and answered, "Oh, that's easy—*when I see my image in it.*"

I want my Savior to see His image reflected in me. And, now I understand that all the suffering is the refining process. I've heard it said that life is a process, and when we have finished processing, we go home. I want to finish well.

Let Me Get Home Before Dark[9]
By Robertson McQuilkin

It's sundown, Lord.
The shadows of my life stretch back
    into the dimness of the years long spent.
I fear not death, for that grim foe betrays himself at last,
    thrusting me forever into life:

Life with You, unsoiled and free.
But I do fear.
I fear the Dark Specter may come too soon—
        or do I mean too late?
That I should end before I finish or
        finish, but not well.
That I should stain your honor, shame your name,
        grieve your loving heart.
Few, they tell me, finish well . . .
Lord, let me get home before dark.

The darkness of a spirit
        grown mean and small, fruit shriveled on the vine,
        bitter to the taste of my companions,
        burden to be borne by those brave few who
        love me still.
No, Lord. Let the fruit grow lush and sweet,
        A joy to all who taste;
Spirit-sign of God at work,
        stronger, fuller, brighter at the end.
Lord, let me get home before dark.

The darkness of tattered gifts,
        rust-locked, half-spent, or ill-spent,
A life that once was used of God
        now set aside.
Grief for glories gone or
Fretting for a task God never gave/
Mourning in the hollow chambers of memory,
Gazing on the faded banners of victories long gone.
Cannot I run well unto the end?
Lord, let me get home before dark.

The outer me decays—
        I do not fret or ask reprieve.
The ebbing strength but weans me from mother earth
        and grows me up for heaven.
I do not cling to shadows cast by mortality.

I do not patch the scaffold lent to build the real, eternal me.
I do not clutch about me my cocoon,
        vainly struggling to hold hostage
        a free spirit pressing to be born.

But will I reach the gate
        in lingering pain, body distorted, grotesque?
Or will it be a mind
        wandering untethered among light
        phantasies or grim terrors?
Of Your grace, Father, I humbly ask . . .
Let me get home before dark.

Chapter Nineteen
I Will Never Leave You Nor Forsake You

For He Himself has said,
"I will never leave you nor forsake you."
Hebrews 13:5b

In My Father's house are many mansions;
if it were not so, I would have told you.
I go to prepare a place for you.
And if I go and prepare a place for you,
I will come again and receive you to Myself;
that where I am, there you may be also.
John 14:2-3

After Mother and Dad died, I tried various methods of coping. I ate chocolate and drank beer—at the same time! It's actually not a bad combination. I called Hospice and asked for help. They pointed me to a support group. I didn't have the energy or motivation to attend. I finally contacted a friend, who is also a counselor, and saw her one time for an hour's session. She pointed out one of the most positive things I have ever heard anyone say about Christ's love for us. She recited

Hebrews 12:2:

> Looking unto Jesus the author and finisher of
> our faith; who *for the joy that was set before*
> *him* endured the cross, despising the shame, and
> is set down at the right hand of the throne of
> God. (KJV. Emphasis mine.)

She asked if I understood what the "joy" was that was set before
Jesus. I admitted that I did not. She said, "It's *us*. It's those of
us who would believe down through the ages!"She explained
that she held a mental picture of Jesus looking down a long
corridor representing time and seeing all of us along the
corridor and being *joyful* in the midst of His misery because of
us! His joy was knowing what His sacrificial atoning death
would accomplish for us who would believe.

And after He laid down His life for us, He arose again
and went home to the Father, promising to return again for us.
That's the good news! It's the good news that empowers us to
overcome any circumstance that life throws at us.

I'm leaving the house. I'm gathering things together and
preparing to leave on an errand. I'm talking to Bandit as I'm
closing the door to my bedroom. He follows me as I
systematically walk through the house closing the doors to
every room that's carpeted. Other than when he was mere
weeks old, Bandit has never, ever peed or pooped in the house.
But he does vomit! So I always close the doors to protect

carpeted areas. Bandit knows the routine. He knows that this means I will be leaving soon. He hopes desperately to go with me, but he knows that the closed doors mean he is staying home.

I'm talking with him and reassuring him that I won't be gone long. "Mommy will be back soon." I say. "I won't be gone long. Mommy would *never* leave you for good. I'll always come back for you because I love you so much." Then it hits me. That's almost exactly what Jesus said when He left this earth—leaving out the "Mommy" part, of course. He said that He would *never* leave us or forsake us and that He would come back again for us. When I say similar words to Bandit, I mean it with all my heart. My eyes brim at the thought of disappointing him by not coming back for him.

Oh, how much more does my God love me! How it must touch His heart to think of coming again to get me soon. Soon, Lord. *Even so, come, Lord Jesus*, Rev. 22:20.

I immediately go back in my mind to a day when my sister and brother-in-law, Matt, and my husband and I were visiting Mother and Daddy. For some reason or other, Matt began sadly reminiscing about the death of their dog Pat years earlier. Pat was a woeful-eyed beagle who came into their family when their son Mark was only a small boy. Pat lived until Mark had finished school and left home for the big city (Atlanta). Many of us who grew up in Georgia left home for

Atlanta after high school to continue our education in one way or another, either through college or through the school of hard knocks out in the business world.

Matt began to describe the day when it became obvious that Pat was nearing his last, and as he described the trauma of making the decision to "put him down," he began to get a little teary. He continued on to detail the inevitable trip to the vet and the fatal injection that sent Pat from this world. With tears spilling down his cheeks, Matt said, "I just couldn't leave him to make that journey alone. I *had* to stay with him. I held him until he drew his last breath."

By now, we were *all* weeping unashamedly—Mother, Sylvia, Matt, Jim and me. At that moment, Daddy walked into the room to be greeted by five faces all drenched with tears. "What happened?" he questioned in alarm—obviously thinking that we must have just gotten some awful news. In unison, we all exclaimed, "Pat!"

"Pat?" Daddy asked, still not having a clue as to what the problem was, and trying to figure out who Pat was and what happened to him or her.

"You know, Pat—Mark's dog," I explained.

"Yeah?"

"Well, Matt was just telling the story of how he stayed with Pat when he was put to sleep."

"Oh."

Now, as I think of that day, I compare Matt's presence with Pat to the Lord's presence with all believers. Scripture tells us that Jesus is seated in Heaven at the right hand of the Father.

> *So then, after the Lord had spoken to them, He was received up into heaven, and sat down at the right hand of God.* Mark 16:19.

And we are, at this very moment, seated in spirit with our Savior in Heaven.

> *[A}nd raised us up together, and made us sit together in the heavenly places in Christ Jesus.* Ephesians 2:6.

When we die, we merely make the transition to the rightful place with our Savior that we already have now in spirit. Jesus our Lord is with us now, and will be with us in the end when we make the journey from here to there. Jesus (in His prayer for all believers just before His crucifixion) promised to be *in* us and to keep us *in* the Father.

> *I do not pray for these alone, but also for those who will believe in Me through their word; that they all may be one, as You, Father, are in Me, and I in You; that they also may be one in Us, that the world may believe that You sent Me.* John 17:20-21.

And, He sent us a Helper (the Holy Spirit), who would witness

167

to us in spirit, so that we would *know* that we belong to Him and that He is with us.

> *And I will pray the Father, and He will give you another Helper, that He may abide with you forever—the Spirit of truth, whom the world cannot receive, because it neither sees Him nor knows Him; but you know Him, for He dwells with you and will be in you. I will not leave you orphans; I will come to you.* John 14:16-18

> *The Spirit Himself bears witness with our spirit that we are children of God.* Romans 8:16

As Matt was with Pat at the moment of Pat's death, so our Lord is with us now and will be with us then—and so He was with Daddy, and with Mother and with Dad. How do I know this? Because He promised never to leave us nor forsake us. Just as Matt promised Pat that he would stay with him until the end, when he carried Pat into the veteranarian's office that awful day. Just so, our Lord is with us to the end—and then beyond the end, *forever.*

Now, I see that although I was not with them, my parents did not go through the valley of the shadow of death alone. The loving Savior was with them, and is with them now, rejoicing in the Heavenly places. Hallelujah!

Chapter Twenty
It Is Enough

I need no other argument
I need no other plea;
It is enough that Jesus died,
And that He died for me.
Excerpt from *My Faith Has Found a Resting Place*
A hymn by Lidie H. Edmunds

Being confident of this very thing,
that He who has begun a good work in you
will complete it until the day of Jesus Christ.
Philippians 1:6

In Your presence is fullness of joy;
At Your right hand are pleasures forevermore.
Psalm 16:11

[W]hatever you do, do all to the glory of God.
1 Corinthians 10:31b

I was saved as a young child, and then "saved again" (some of you can relate) as a thirty-two-year-old woman after much wandering trying to "find myself." So even from the early days of my spiritual walk, I have been intimately familiar with the wilderness.

When I was first saved, God and His love and salvation seemed so uncomplicated. I remember as an eight-year-old going to my daddy with questions about whether or not I could "join the church." Daddy responded by asking if I believed in Jesus. He was, rightfully, concerned as to whether this young daughter of his really understood what it meant to be saved and to "join the church." In my innocence, I replied, "Daddy, *everybody* believes in Jesus!" I honestly didn't know that there were people who did not.

In my hometown, things were pretty fundamental—at least they were in my own young mind. For instance, I thought that mowing your lawn on Sunday was a mortal sin, and I was shocked to discover that some people actually did do yard work on Sundays.

When my friend Dotsie joined the church, I suddenly felt a desire within myself to follow suit. It seemed like such a simple matter. I believed in Jesus, so I should be a part of the church. Besides, everyone had commented on how sweet Dotsie had looked as she gazed intently into the preacher's eyes and declared her belief in the Lord. I wanted the same kind of recognition, and I harbored a secret desire to participate in Communion. I always felt slighted when the grape juice and crackers glided by me at just about eye level as my mother passed the brightly polished brass plates into the hands of the next worshiper. Why should I be left out?

So one bright Sunday morning, I marched down the aisle of the First Baptist Church of Fitzgerald and professed my faith before God and all the congregation. I was careful to look intently into the preacher's eyes. After all, I was in competition with Dotsie!

As I grew up, I developed an unsettling awareness that my motives for becoming a part of our church were not the best, and I began to question whether I actually had been saved or not. Being as yet unfamiliar with the promise of Philippians 1:6, I had no idea that God had honored my childish confession of my belief in Jesus Christ and had begun a "good work" in me and would complete it. I didn't know that He alone is the "author and finisher" of my faith, Hebrews 12:2. That he *gave* me the very faith I needed to trust Him and that He would continue to mature that faith until, as He said on the cross, "It is *finished*!" John 19:30 (emphasis mine).

There were many revivals throughout my youth and early adulthood where I "rededicated" my life to Jesus Christ—usually at the urging of some revival preacher pointing an accusatory finger into the congregation and insisting that there were some of us who, though church members, had never been saved and who were just playing at Christianity. Each time such an indictment was made, I flushed with shame and felt that, without a doubt, I had been found out—that the evangelist was pointing his chastening finger right at me! So the inevitable rededication would follow. I've long ago lost track of how many times I rededicated my life to the Lord.

By the time I reached my mid-twenties, I had thoroughly messed up my life. I was in a seemingly hopeless, loveless marriage that had produced two beautiful young sons. I had little time for them, however, because I loved the party life. I worked as a bookkeeper in an office all week. On weekends, my husband and I would often hire a babysitter to stay the entire weekend so that we could ride motorcycles and hang out on the beach during the day, and then drink and dance at night into the wee hours of the morning. This party life eventually led to my husband's alcoholism and our divorce. I was divorced only six months before I remarried. I married a Christian man who began to see that I had some significant emotional and spiritual problems.

One night, as he sat up in the living room praying for me, Jim felt led to wake me (at about 3:00 a.m.!) and ask me to pray. He said, "I don't know what you are supposed to pray, but the Lord has impressed on me that I need to ask you to get out of bed and on your knees." I was too sleepy to argue at that insufferable hour, so I simply obeyed. I was groggy and sleepy, but I climbed out of bed and onto my knees. Once I was there, and once I called out to my Heavenly Father, I realized what a sorry mess I had made of my life, and I simply asked Him to take over and fix it.

I was immediately flooded with peace. I crawled back into bed and slept like a baby. When I awakened the next morning, I was at first concerned that the peace might be gone—that maybe it was all a dream. But the peace remained. And it has continued to remain with me, at some conscious or subconscious level, ever since. I say "subconscious" because at times I'm not all that aware of a sensation of peace. At times, my life seems really troubled, but there remains a deep tranquility that surface troubles don't seem to penetrate.

But the "wilderness" remains a constant as well, and from time to time I wander around in it again. It's always when I have neglected my prayer life. I have wandered away and I don't even talk to God. It's difficult to maintain a relationship when one party is not speaking to the other. You would think I would figure this out. But I don't. I go back into the wilderness, and I don't find my way out again until I start talking to my Heavenly Father—Abba, Daddy—God about it. Immediately when I come to Him, the dark wilderness retreats. It has to. For *God is Light and in Him is no darkness at all* (1 John 1:5), and darkness has no association with light.

For what fellowship has righteousness with lawlessness? And what communion has light with darkness? 2 Cor. 6:14b.

173

As I sit here writing this last chapter, it occurs to me that, at age sixty-three, I still don't yet know what I want to be. This morning I talked with the Lord about it. I have talked with Him often about this because it concerns me more and more as I begin to view my life from the end rather than from the beginning. As a youth, one views life from the beginning, seeing one's earthly existence all ahead ever pressing forward like a long endless journey. But at some point, one starts to see life from its termination—what have I done so far, what do I hope to accomplish before my final curtain is drawn?

I'm not sure exactly when my perspective changed, but at some point, I began seeing my life from its conclusion. Perhaps it was a natural transformation following my mother's death.

When one's last remaining parent dies, there is a sense of loss not only of the parent but also of a curious sense of protection. As long as at least one parent is living, there seems to be (at least an illusion of) an "insulation" of sorts between the adult child (regardless of age) and death—a type of hierarchy, if you will, safekeeping the child one step removed from his/her own expiration. Upon the death of the last parent, however, the perceived insulation is gone. Following my mother's death, I realized that I had lost not only my parents but also the supposed buffer separating me from my own demise.

Contemplating one's own mortality leads to all kinds of

self-examination. Have I lived well in the past? Am I living well now? Where am I going from here? What am I going to do with the time I have remaining? How can I best use that time? And, most important, how would *God* have me use the time? Now that I'm viewing my life from the end, I've been feeling a certain pressure to accomplish whatever it is that I'm going to accomplish before I go Home.

I went to the Lord with it this morning and just flat out asked Him what He expected me to accomplish before I leave this earth. As I was asking, I noticed Bandit on the floor in front of me doing what he does best—sleeping! And I felt a surge of joy just to have him there in the room with me. Almost immediately a still, quiet voice in my mind said, "What do you expect Bandit to accomplish?"

I answered, "Nothing. I just enjoy his company. I just want him to love me as I love him." Maybe the Lord doesn't use the word, "Bingo!" but I'm almost certain I heard it. Wow!

My mind went to Jesus' response in Matthew 22:37-38 when a lawyer asked, "Which is the great commandment?" Jesus replied, *"You shall love the Lord your God with all your heart, with all your soul, and with all your mind. This is the first and great commandment."* The Westminster Shorter Catechism points out: *The chief end of man is to glorify God and enjoy him forever.* (WSC 1). That's it! That's what we are supposed to "accomplish"—love God, enjoy Him and His great love, and bring glory to Him. (My interpretation of bringing "glory" to Him: Try our best not to embarrass Him—by claiming to belong to Him and then acting dishonorably, bringing shame to His holy name. I believe that if we truly love Him, our actions will follow His plan—at least most of the time. We may mess up from time to time, but when we do, we are truly sorry, and we tell Him we are.)

Please understand that I recognize that many people are specially called into service as ministers, missionaries, evangelists, and other types of ministry. (Ephesians 4:11). But our ultimate purpose is to *love God* because He loves us so much, and to *enjoy* Him. I understand this now because I love a small dog who delights me so much just in loving me in return. There's no pressure on him to perform. He has not earned my "grace"—my love. He merely leaps into the air for joy whenever I come through the front door. He doesn't even have to see my face. As soon as he senses my presence, he goes into paroxysms of sheer ecstasy. I truly believe it is that kind of joy that the Lord seeks in His children. Just to delight in His presence. That's my purpose, until or unless I receive a higher call from Him. Is it not awesome that God, who created the heavens, the earth, the universe, and untold galaxies and universes yet to be discovered—is it not awesome that this God loves me, loves you, and desires our love in return? He wants to fellowship with us. He wants to hang out with us. He desires our joy in His presence.

And then there are cats . . . . Cats don't even have the decency to celebrate their master's presence. Cats are aloof, self-absorbed, lazy, indolent—yet their owners love them completely. I used to have cats before I fell in love with dogs. I loved my cats fully as much as I have ever loved any dog. Yet none of my cats ever lifted a single toe in even the slightest attempt to please me. All they ever did was purr when *I* pleased *them*. Did I love them any less for being cats instead of dogs? Goodness, no. I loved them for being cats! They were created to be cats, for Heaven's sake. So I didn't expect the adoration that one receives from a dog. I expected to be ignored and merely tolerated. My joy was to pick up my cat and hold it and hear its contented purring in my ear.

In this busy world, where I often run around so preoccupied that I am sometimes barely aware of God's presence in my life, it is comforting to know that God loves us even when we are self-absorbed and merely purr from time to time in response to His great love. I am at peace.

> *Surely I have composed and quieted my soul;*
> *Like a weaned child rests against his mother,*
> *My soul is like a weaned child within me.* Psalm 131:2

Yet there remains in my mind this "end-of-life-as-I-know-it" thing. I saw a puzzle in a little gift shop section of Ace

Hardware one day. The picture on the box cover immediately caught my eye and called out to me. It was the picture of a long banquet table set with many places as far as the eye could see. Above the table were great, mighty, robed arms reaching out to "whosoever will," inviting us to come to the feast. This was shortly after Mother and Dad passed away, so when I saw this picture, my eyes immediately filled with tears, and I nearly completely lost my composure right there in the middle of Ace Hardware. I could practically see my parents sitting at that table along with other friends and family who have gone before. My heart leapt at the thought of joining them at the Lord's banquet. I thought of the scripture in the Bible's love song—the Song of Solomon: *He brought me to the banqueting house and his banner over me was love.* Song of Solomon 2:4. He called *me* to celebrate in a joyous feast with *Him*, the Creator, and His banner flying over that banquet is *love*. Can you imagine?

There was an email circling around in cyberspace for a while about a man who was facing death and who inquired of his doctor about coming to grips with his imminent demise.

> A sick man turned to his doctor, as he was preparing to leave the examination room and said, "Doctor, I am afraid to die. Tell me what lies on the other side."
>
> Very quietly, the doctor said, "I don't know."
> "You don't know? You, a Christian man, do not

know what is on the other side?"

The doctor was holding the handle of the door. On the other side came a sound of scratching and whining, and as he opened the door, a dog sprang into the room and leaped on him with an eager show of gladness.

Turning to the patient, the doctor said, "Did you notice my dog? He's never been in this room before. He didn't know what was inside. He knew nothing except that his master was here, and when the door opened, he sprang in without fear. I know little of what is on the other side of death, but I do know one thing. . . . I know my Master is there, and that is enough."

Dear friends, *it is enough!*

Epilogue

I have come to terms with certain facts. Suffering, death and grief are a part of life as we know it here on earth. Terrible things entered our sphere with Adam and Eve's original sin in the Garden of Eden. God can, but does not often, intervene in the natural processes of this fallen world. I have come to understand that the goal is a life lived within God's will—a life lived well and finished well.

I got the call on Tuesday, two days before Thanksgiving in 2005. The drive to Georgia would be a long one, but I knew I had to go. I had to honor a friend, a man for whom I had great respect. The call let me know that Ron Wiggins had lost his fight against cancer. He had put up a brave fight. He had lost the battle but won the war. He had finished well.

Approximately two years prior, Ron had been diagnosed with an aggressive form of melanoma located behind his right eye. The eye had to be removed. For a few weeks, Ron wore an eye patch which gave him a rakish appearance—sort of like a handsome pirate. Eventually, however, he was fitted with a prosthetic eye. It was attached to tendons in such a way that it actually moved in partnership with his left eye. The natural movement gave the prosthesis a more normal look. Yet it was obvious that there was something different about the "eye."

Friends and family clung to the hope that the cancer had not invaded other organs. It had . . . and it continued to do so.

I had met Ron years earlier as a business associate. I considered him to be the epitome of a "Southern gentleman." In my mind's ear, I can still hear his soft, decidedly Southern, voice.

Ron was one of the most hospitable people I have ever known. In better days, Jim and I had spent happy times with him and his sweet wife, Sammie. They lived in Carrollton, Georgia—about an eight-hour drive from our home in Ellenton, Florida. We had spent weekends in their home and at a vacation lodge Ron owned with his lifelong friend, and golfing buddy, Walter Duke. The lodge is located on a large manmade lake nestled in three hundred acres of Georgia pine trees.

Because of previous commitments, Jim was precluded from going with me to the funeral. My son, Alan, also a tremendous fan of Ron's, agreed to go with me and drive. Since the Thanksgiving holiday was fast approaching, the family decided to make immediate arrangements and hold the service promptly—the day after Ron's death. Even on such short notice, hundreds of people came to the visitation service and funeral—a testimony to the life Ron lived and the kind of man he was.

Oh, to be so well-loved and remembered. What a

legacy! Ron finished well.

Alan and I left within hours after the phone call, arriving in Carrollton in the wee hours of Wednesday morning. When we arrived at the visitation service that afternoon, we immediately spotted Sammie, Walter, and Walter's son Wade, who also had been a close friend of Ron's. After offering our condolences, we noticed that there was a video of special moments in Ron's life playing on a television placed in an anteroom. I can only imagine the love and cooperation it took for family and friends to be able to pull that video together so quickly. Seeing Ron's face on the screen brought a lump to my throat and fresh tears to my eyes. I stole a look at Alan and saw that it had a similar effect on him.

The video showed us things we had not known about Ron—*e.g.* he had been a highschool and college football hero. He looked out at us from the video, a baby-faced young man in a football uniform. He had a thick, full head of hair—quite a contrast to the nearly bald Ron we had known.

Ron was only fifty-four years old. I venture to say that in the last two years of his life, he probably grew spiritually more than in all the other fifty-two.

Until the cancer invaded Ron's world, I had not known much about his relationship with the Lord. We were business acquaintances who, over the years, became friends—but friends who talked business, seldom ever venturing into our personal lives or beliefs. When told the seriousness of his condition, Ron experienced all the classic steps of grief—denial, initially, then fear, followed by negotiation (with God), and finally acceptance.

We became spiritual pen pals through that phenomenal communication tool—e-mail. Ron's emotional turmoil (all the highs and lows of it) spilled out through his e-mails. I, along with many of his other friends, encouraged him to look to Jesus, the Great Physician. We also encouraged him to seek all forms of medical help that made sense to him—conventional and alternative as well. We prayed that the Lord would spare his life, either miraculously or through some type of medical treatment.

I felt certain in my spirit that Ron would be healed. I think he also strongly believed that he would be healed. His healing came in a way I don't think anyone really expected. It was a spiritual healing, not a physical one. The more the disease raged against his physical life, the stronger Ron's spiritual life became. As detailed in his later e-mails, he reached the point where he could say as Paul did long ago:

For to me to live is Christ, and to die is gain.
Philippians 1:21

On November 22, 2005, Ron gained his place in Heaven with his Creator and the Savior he loved. Earth's loss was

Heaven's gain.

In the months just prior to his death, Ron became an inspiration for myriads of people, as he spoke with friends, relatives, church groups and various audiences urging others to find the peace he had found in totally relying on God. I am forever changed because of Ron's life and his testimony. I, and countless others, are eternally transformed by a life finished well.

Take a few moments right now to think about your friends and family. Contemplate how different, and how much poorer, your life would have been without these dear ones.

Life is a journey. It is made better (or worse) by the family into which we are born and by the friends and associates we choose. It is vitally important to choose your friends and life partners wisely from the very early moments of your life. Your life will most definitely be shaped and defined by the companions you keep. And, here's where it gets scary, your friends and relatives' lives will be forever impacted by their having associated with and loved *you*. What kind of relationships are you making? What kind of legacy are you leaving? Will you finish well?

We are all responsible for the footprints we leave on each others' lives. It is imperative that we finish well. Paul the Apostle finished well. Just prior to his death, he wrote from a Roman prison to his friend and co-laborer Timothy:

I have fought the good fight, I have finished the race, I have kept the faith. 2 Timothy 4:7

Where are you in your life's journey? Just starting out? Almost done?

Where are you in your spiritual journey? Perhaps you have a sweet relationship with the Father/Creator through His only begotten son, Jesus Christ. Perhaps, on the other hand, you don't have that relationship and don't know how to acquire it, but you would like to.

If that describes you, I encourage you to look to God's word for answers. If you prayerfully ask Him to reveal the truth to you, He will. The scriptures are clear that three days after Jesus was crucified, He rose from the dead—as He had predicted He would—and He was seen by large numbers of people before ascending to the Father.

> *For I delivered to you first of all that which I also received: that Christ died for our sins according to the Scriptures, and that He was buried, and that He rose again the third day according to the Scriptures, and that He was seen by Cephas, then by the twelve. After that He was seen by over five hundred brethren at once, of whom the greater part remain to the present, but some have fallen asleep. After that He was seen by James, then by all the apostles. Then last of all He was seen by me also, as by one born out of due time.* I Corinthians 15:3-8.

He has prepared an amazing home for you.

> *In My Father's house are many mansions; if it were not so, I would have told you. I go to prepare a place for you. And if I go and prepare a place for you, I will come again and receive you to Myself; that where I am, there you may be also.* John 14:2-3

The way to God is astonishingly simple and is stated plainly in scripture. First of all, we are assured that God rewards those who earnestly seek Him.

> *But without faith it is impossible to please Him, for he who comes to God must believe that He is, and that he is a rewarder of those who diligently seek Him.* Hebrews 11:6

But we are told that sin keeps us from Him and that we have all sinned and need His forgiveness.

> *For all have sinned and fall short of the glory of God.* Romans 3:23

There is a price to be paid for sin, and that price is death.

> *For the wages of sin is death, but the gift of God is eternal life in Jesus Christ our Lord.* Romans 6:23

The price to be paid for sin is death. God decreed it and,

because He is a Holy God, He cannot go against His own law. We would each have to pay the price for our sins unless somehow someone else could pay the price for us—unless someone could *redeem* us.

> *But when the fullness of the time had come, God sent forth His Son, born of a woman, born under the law, to redeem those who were under the law, that we might receive the adoption as sons. And because you are sons, God has sent forth the Spirit of His Son into your hearts, crying out, "Abba, Father!" Therefore you are no longer a slave but a son, and if a son, then an heir of God through Christ.* Galatians 4:4-7

Someone as sinful as we are could not redeem us. We needed a perfect, sinless savior.

> *For He made Him who knew no sin to be sin for us, that we might become the righteousness of God in Him.* 2 Corinthians 5:21

Since *all* have sinned, there was no one to pay the price. Therefore, God Himself sent His only son to earth to be a sinless sacrifice for the sins of the world—my sins, and yours.

> *For God so loved the world that he gave his only begotten Son that whoever believes in him should not perish but have everlasting life.* John 3:16

But God demonstrates His own love toward us, in that while we were still sinners, Christ died for us. Romans 5:8

But He was wounded for our transgressions, He was bruised for our iniquities; the chastisement for our peace was upon Him, and by His stripes we are healed. All we like sheep have gone astray; we have turned, every one, to his own way; and the Lord has laid on Him the iniquity of us all. Isaiah 53:5-6

Through God's Son, we have the *free gift* of eternal life with Him in Heaven. We can do nothing to earn it; it is a *gift.*

For by grace you have been saved through faith, and that not of yourselves; it is the gift of God, not of works, lest anyone should boast. Ephesians 2:8-9

He who has the Son has life; he who does not have the Son of God does not have life. 1 John 5:12

But now is Christ risen from the dead, and become the firstfruits of them that slept. For since by man came death, by man came also the resurrection of the dead. For as in Adam all die, even so in Christ shall all be made alive. I Corinthians 15:20-22

Jesus is the *only* way.

> *Jesus said to him, "I am the way, the truth, and the life. No one comes to the Father except through Me."* John 14:6

> *[H]ow shall we escape if we neglect so great a salvation, which at the first began to be spoken by the Lord, and was confirmed to us by those who heard Him. . .?* Hebrews 2:3

A gift isn't a gift until it's *received*. As long as it remains in the bearer's hands, the intended receiver does not *have* the gift. Are you ready to reach out and take God's gift? It's as easy as praying a simple prayer:

Dear God, my Abba (Daddy),

I want to spend eternity with You. I need peace, and I need forgiveness. I turn from my old life and ask You for a new life. Fill me with Your Spirit so that I will be able to live in accordance with Your plans and purposes for me.

I accept the gift of Your Son, Jesus Christ, who took the form of a servant, came into this world and died for me so that I might be forgiven of my sins and have eternal life with You. Please take me from darkness into light and teach me about You. I want to live well and finish well.

In Jesus name,
Amen. (So be it!)

If you sincerely prayed such a simple prayer accepting God's free gift of salvation through His son Jesus Christ, you have become a child of God and my brother or sister in the Lord. Your place with God is secure. No one can take it from you—you are born again; you can't be unborn. You can rest in your redemption.

> *My sheep hear my voice, and I know them, and they follow me: And I give unto them eternal life; and they shall never perish, neither shall any man pluck them out of my hand. My Father, which gave them me, is greater than all; and no man is able to pluck them out of my Father's hand. I and my Father are one.*
> John 10 :27-30

Now ask the Lord to show you a church where you can worship and serve and fellowship with other believers. Get into God's word, the Bible, and listen to what He has to say to you through His word. You will be amazed at the insights He will give you as you truly seek to know Him.

God bless you.

Welcome to the family!

NOTES

Chapter Three – Seeing God Through Puppy Eyes

1. Gire, Ken. *Windows of the Soul*, Grand Rapids Michigan, Zondervan, 1996.

Chapter Four – Taming the 2-lb. Beast

2. Hester, Benny; Parenti, John. *When God Ran* © 1985 Word Music, LLC. All Rights Reserved. Used by Permission.

Chapter Seven – Sleeping Secure In His Love

3. Jernigan, Dennis. *When the Night Is Falling* © 1991 Shepherd's Heart Music, Inc. All Rights Reserved. Used by Permission of Alfred Publishing Co., Inc.

Chapter Eight – Learning Love's Language

4. Youngblood, Ronald F., et al. *Nelson's New Illustrated Bible Dictionary*, Nashville, Thomas Nelson Publishers, 1995.

Chapter Thirteen – The God of All Comfort

5. Milan, Cesar. *Cesar's Way*, New York, Harmony Books, 2006.

NOTES

Chapter Fifteen – Freedom!

6.   George, Bob. *Growing In Grace*, Eugene, OR, Harvest House Publishers, 1991, p. 167-168.

Chapter Seventeen – God Bless You, Sweetheart

7.   Gire, Ken. *Windows of the Soul*, Grand Rapids Michigan, Zondervan, 1996, p. 11-12.

Chapter Eighteen –   To Know Him and the Fellowship of His Sufferings

8.   Gire, Ken. *Moments with the Savior*, Grand Rapids, Michigan, Zondervan, 1998, p. 389.

9.   *Let Me Get Home Before Dark*
a prayer shared by Robertson McQuilkin, President Emeritus, Columbia International University. Used by Permission.

To order
What My Dog Taught Me About God
visit **www.booksbylemontree.com**